MW00532171

Our Great and Glorious God

by

Jonathan Edwards

(taken from the sermons and miscellanies)

Compiled and Edited by Dr. Don Kistler

Soli Deo Gloria Publications
. . . for instruction in righteousness . . .

Soli Deo Gloria Publications
A division of Soli Deo Gloria Ministries, Inc.
P. O. Box 451, Morgan PA 15064
(412) 221-1901/Fax (412) 221-1902
www.SDGbooks.com

*

*

ISBN 1-57358-153-4

Library of Congress Cataloging-in-Publication Data

Edwards, Jonathan, 1703-1758.
  Our great and glorious God / by Jonathan Edwards; compiled and edited
by Don Kistler.
     p. cm.
  ISBN 1-57358-153-4 (alk. paper)
  1. God–Attributes. I. Kistler, Don. II. Title.
  BT130 .E39 2003
  231–dc21
                                              2003009912

Contents

The Existence of God *Ponderous*   1

The Nature of God   11

The Grace of God   26

The Sovereignty of God *Powerful in logic*   39

The Decrees of God *" "*   54

The Glory of God   85

The Wisdom of God *Extensive + Thorough 360 pages!*   95

The Justice of God   166

Heaven Is God's House   198

The Existence of God

We know there was being from eternity; and this being must be intelligent, for how could our mind refuse to believe that there should be being from all eternity without its being conscious to itself that it was. That there should be something from all eternity, and yet not know all that while that anything is, is really a contradiction. We may see it to be so though we do not know how to express it. For in what respect does anything have a being when it is not conscious of its own being? And in what respect does anything have a being that neither angels nor men nor any other created intelligence know nothing of, but only as God knows it to be? Not at all, any more than there are sounds where none hears or colors where none sees. Thus, for instance, suppose that there is a room in which no one is; no one sees in that room, there is no created intelligence. The things in the room have no being in any other way than as God is conscious of them, for there is no color, nor any sound, nor any shape

God is a necessary being, because it's a contradiction to suppose Him not to be. A being is a necessary being whose nonentity is a contradiction. Absolute nothing is the essence of all contradiction. But being in order is all that we call God, who is, and there is none else besides Him.

It is acknowledged by all to be self-evident that nothing can begin to be without cause. Neither can we prove it in any other way than by explaining it. When understood, it is a truth that irresistably will have place in the assent. Thus, if we suppose a time wherein there was nothing, a body will not, of its own accord, begin to be. The understanding abhors that something should be when there was no manner of reason why it was. So it is equally self-evident that a being cannot begin to be, as to the manner of its being, without a cause, as that when a body has been perfectly at rest that it should begin to move without any reason, either within itself or without. So that, "because it just happened" will not satisfy the mind at all. The mind asks what was the reason. So it is equally self-evident, if equally understood, that there must be a reason why a body should be after one manner and not after another. Thus, if a body is a moving body, there must be some reason or cause why it is a moving body and not a resting body. It must be because of something, otherwise there is something without a cause, such as much as when a body starts into being of itself. Suppose there are two globes: the one is a moving globe, the other is a resting one. The mind asks why the one moves and the other rests. It is natural to the mind to say something is the reason why this body moves and not the other; and if it should be said, "No, there is not, nor ever was, any reason or cause why this being should move more than why the other should," the mind immediately returns, "If there is no reason why one should move more than the other, why then does one move and the other rest?" It abhors the supposition that there is none. So if two bodies are of different figures, there is some reason why this is of this shape and that of the other. So when one body moves with one degree of velocity and another of another; when one body is of one bigness and another of another; when one body moves with one direction and another of another; one rests on this place, another, another, it is exceedingly evident that there must be some cause or other for these things. Wherefore now I ask the question of the different bodies in the world: Why is this body in this place and not in any or some other, and why is this body of such dimensions and not of others? Why is this body of this figure and that of that, and why does this move and that rest? Why does this body move with just such a degree of velocity, and why do the planets move west to east and not from east to west? Something must be the reason for it. If it be said it is so because it was so from all eternity, or because there was such a succession of alterations from eternity as to cause it to be so now, how did it come to be so from all eternity? If there can be absolutely no reason or cause why it should be so any more than why it should be infinite other ways, then I say it wasn't so from eternity. And why was there not another succession of alterations from eternity so as to cause another sort of alteration now?

It is evident that none of the creatures, none of the beings that we behold, are the first principle of their own action; but all alterations follow in a chain from other alterations. Now, therefore, there must necessarily be something in itself active so as that it is the very first beginning of its own actions, or some necessary being that has been the cause of all the rest, which cannot be matter since it does not have the nature of matter.

The existence of our own souls, which we know more immediately than anything, is an argument of exceedingly glaring evidence for the existence of a God. Our souls were not always there, but they are wonderful beings, certainly exceeding in contrivance everything that is seen or can be seen with eyes. They are pieces of workmanship so curious and of such amazing contrivance that their operation infinitely exceeds those of any machines that are seen. Let us consider what has been done and what is daily done by human souls. What strange contrivance is this, to take in the sun, moon, and stars, and the whole universe, and bring all distant things together, and to make past and future things present, to move the body after such a manner, to produce such strange effects on other souls and in the corporeal world! If our souls are material machines, certainly they are so curious that none will deny that they are the effect of contrivance. Let them be created immediately, or let them be by propagation, the contrivance is wonderful. What contrivance is necessary to make such machines that will produce and propagate other such machines in an infinite succession! And if they be not material, whence are they if not from a superior immaterial being? And if we say our souls existed from eternity, who is it orders it so that upon every generation a soul shall be brought and united to such a parcel of matter? Or if we say our souls existed in the bodies from eternity, existing one within another in infinitum, who contrived this matter so?

If the atheist will not acknowledge any great order and regularity in the corporeal world, he must acknowledge that there is in spirits, in minds, which will be as much an argument for a contriver as if the contrivance was in bodies. He must acknowledge that reason, wisdom, and contrivance are regular actions. But they are the actions of spirits. Many of the works of men are wonderfully regular, but certainly no more regular than the contrivance that was the author of them. And who made those beings that they should act as regularly as the nicest machines of men? Did such nice beings come into existence by chance or were they not the effect of a superior contrivance?

Hence we see that all man's works and human inventions and artifices are arguments of the existence of God, as well as those that are more immediately the works of God, for they are only the regular actings of God's works. When we walk in stately cities or admire curious machines and inventions, let us argue the wisdom of God as well as of the immediate contrivers. For those spirits who were the contrivers are the most wonderful contrivances.

The mere exertion of a new thought is a certain proof of a god. For certainly there is something that immediately produces and upholds that thought. Here is a new thing, and there is a necessity of a cause. It is not in antecedent thoughts, for they are vanished and gone; they are past, and what is past does not exist.

That sweet intimation and sort of inward testimony that men have, upon occasion, of the being of a God, and which is in the mind of all men, however they may endeavor to root it out, is this: First, arguing for the being of a god according to the natural powers from everything we are conversant with is short and easy, and what we naturally fall into. Second, it appears decorous and orderly that it should be so, and that natural inclination that persons have to excellence and order does, as it were, prejudice in favor of it. When we suffer great injustice, we look to some superior being to set things right, because there is a great resistance of the soul against that sort of indecorum and we do not know how to believe that injustice should be done without ever being mended. It is so abhorrent to nature. So when we have done good or evil, we naturally expect from some superior being reward or punishment. Third, there is a habit of the mind in reasoning. We are wont every day, from our very infancy, to argue causes from effects after the same manner, in general. And we have such a habit that we believe this or that without standing to argue about it. Thus we do in many other cases, and as long as we are thus forced to judge in other things continually, it will return upon us inevitably when we think anything about the being of a God.

The being of God may be argued from the desirableness and need of it. This we see in all nature everywhere, that great necessities are supplied. We should be miserably off without our light in the night, and we have the moon and stars. In India and Egypt they are very much without rain, and they have the floods of the Ganges and the Nile and great deserts. In Greenland the sun's rays are exceedingly oblique, and it is above the horizon so much the longer to make it up. Moles have poor eyes, and they have little occasion for them. Beasts are without reason, and they are guided by instinct that supplies its place as well. Men are without natural weapons to fight, and they have reason and hands to make weapons. The young of insects are not able to provide for themselves, nor do their dams take care of them, but they, by instinct, are laid where they have their food round about them. Camels are forced, being in dry countries, to go long without water, and they have a large vessel within them which, being filled, supplies them a long time. So it is in everything. Therefore we cannot think there should be so great and essential and universal and eternal a defect that there should be no wise, just, and good being to govern the world, that the miseries among reasonable creatures, both through the defect of nature and through wickedness and injustice (which are infinitely more than in all the rest of the creation), can never be relieved.

If we should suppose that the world is eternal, yet the beauty, contrivance, and useful disposition of the world would no less strongly conclude for the being of an intelligent author. It will appear in this question: If we should see such a poem as Virgil's *Aeneid*, would it satisfy us if we were told that it was from eternity, transcribed from copy to copy (though we supposed that a succession of men had actually existed from eternity), if we were told that it was made by the casual falling of ink on paper?

The being of God is evident by the Scriptures, and the Scriptures themselves are an evidence of their own divine authority, after the same manner as the existence of a human thinking being is evident by the motions, behavior, and speech of a body of a human form and contexture, and that the body is animated by a rational mind. For we know this no otherwise than by the consistency, harmony, and concurrence of the train of actions and sounds, and that according to all that we can suppose to be in a rational mind. These are a clear evidence of an understanding and design that is the origin of those actions. So there is that wondrous, universal harmony and consent and concurrence in the Scriptures: such a universal appearance of a wonderful glorious design, such stamps everywhere of exalted and divine wisdom, majesty, and holiness in matter, manner, contexture, and aim—that the evidence is the same that the Scriptures are the word and work of a divine mind to one who is thoroughly acquainted with them as it is that the words and actions of an understanding man are from a rational mind to one who has, for a long time, been his familiar acquaintance.

When an infant first comes into the world and sees persons and hears their voices, before it is acquainted with their action and voice, before it has so much comprehension of them as to see something of their consistence, harmony, and concurrence, makes no distinction between their bodies and other things, their motion and sounds, and the motions and sounds of inanimate things. But as its comprehension increases, the understanding and design begin to appear. So it is with men who are so little acquainted with the Scriptures as infants are with the actions of human bodies. They cannot see any evidence of a divine mind as the origin of it because they do not have enough comprehension to apprehend the harmony and wisdom of it.

The only reason why we are ready to object against the absolute, indivisible, unconditional necessity of God's being is that we are ready to conceive that there might be a second option. We are ready to say, "Why could not there have been nothing," as if this were an option. But it is because of the miserableness of our conceptions that we are ready to imagine any such supposition. It is just talk whether there is any such supposition or not unless we knew what nothing was. But we cannot have any such knowledge because there is no such thing as nothing.

God is a necessary being, as it is impossible but that God should exist because there is no other way. There is no second to make a disjunction. There is nothing else supposable. To illustrate this by one of God's attributes, take eternity. It is absolutely necessary that eternity should be, and it is because there is no other way. To say eternity or not eternity is no disjunction, because there is no such thing to make a proposition about as no eternity. Nor can we, in our minds, make any such supposition as not any eternity. We may seem to make such a supposition in words, but it is no supposition because the words have no sense in thought to answer them. They are words as much without any sense in thought that they should signify as these: a crooked straight line, or a square circle, or a six-angled triangle. If we suppose that there is no eternity, it is the same as if we should say or suppose that there never was any such thing as duration, which is a contradiction, for the word "never" implies eternity, and it is the same as to say there never was any such a duration from all eternity. So that in the very doubting of the thing we affirm it.

It is from the exceedingly imperfect notion that we have of the nature or essence of God, and because we cannot think of it but we must think of it far otherwise than it is, that the difficulty in our mind of conceiving of God's existing without a cause arises. It is repugnant to the nature of our souls, and what our faculties utterly refuse to admit, that anything that is capable of being one part of a proper disjunction should exist and be as it is, rather than not exist or exist otherwise without causes. The notions we have of the divine nature are so imperfect that our imperfect idea admits of a disjunction, for whatsoever is not absolutely perfect does so. In everything that is imperfect there is dependence or contingent existence implied in the nature of it, and we can conceive of its being a part of a disjunction. There is a "thus" and an "otherwise" in the case. As soon as we have descended one step below absolute perfection, possibility ceases to be simple; it divides and becomes manifold. Thus, for instance, we cannot conceive of God without attributing succession to Him, but that notion brings along with it contingent existence, and introduces with it a manifold possibility. There is nothing that exists in a successive duration but it will necessarily follow from thence that it is entirely possible that it might exist infinite other ways than it does, and that it might not exist at all.

It is a contradiction to suppose that being itself should not be. If anyone says, "No, there may be nothing," he supposes at the same time that nothing has a being. And indeed nothing, when we speak properly, or when the word has any meaning, i.e., when we speak of nothing in contradiction to some particular being has truly a being.

We have all reason to think that this First Cause of all things, that is the cause of all perception and intelligence in the world, is not only not an unintelligent, unknowing, and insensible being, but that He is infinitely the most intelligent and sensible being of all; that He is more perceiving than any; that His perception is so much more sensible, lively, and perfect that created minds are, in comparison to Him, like dead, senseless, unperceiving substances; and that He infinitely more exceeds them in the sensibility and life and height (if I may so speak) of His perception than the sun exceeds the planets in the intensive degree of its brightness, as well as the bulk or extent of its shining disk. And as He is more sensible, so He is, as I may express it, more voluntary than created minds. He acts more of Himself, infinitely more purely active, and in no respect passive.

There is a reason to be given why God should have a being. The reason is because there is no other way. There is nothing else supposable to be put with the being of God as the other part of the disjunction. If there is, it is absolute and universal nothing. A supposition of something is a supposition of the being of God. It does not only presuppose it, but it implies it. It implies it not only consequently but immediately. God is the sum of all being, and there is no being without His being. All things are in Him, and He in all. But there is no such thing supposable as an absolute universal nothing. We talk nonsense when we suppose any such thing. We deceive ourselves when we think we do in our minds suppose it, or when we imagine we suppose it to be possible. What we do when we go to think of absolute nihility (if I may so speak) is only to remove one thing to make way for and suppose another. In this case, there is no such thing as two parts of a disjunction. When we are come to being in general, we come to one single point without a disjunction. Therefore, God is because there is no other way. God is because there is nothing else to make a supposition of.

The Nature of God

The Holiness of God: God's holiness is His having a due, meet, and proper regard to everything, and therefore consists mainly and preeminently in His infinite regard or love for Himself. He is infinitely the greatest and most excellent being, and therefore a meet and proper regard for Himself is infinitely greater than for all other beings. Now as He is, as it were, the sum of all being, and all other positive existence is but a communication from Him, hence it will follow that a proper regard for Himself is the sum of His regard.

The righteousness of a judge consists in his judging according to law, or to the rule of judgment which has been fixed by rightful legislators, especially if the law and rule of judgment fixed are good, whatever good principles influenced the legislators in making such laws, whether justice or goodness and mercy. But God, in the blessings He adjudges to his people, judges according to the fixed rule of judgment which is His covenant. God shows His holiness by fulfilling His promises to His people. God's faithfulness is part of His holiness, and this is what is meant by righteousness.

The Justice of God: It appears plain enough that an omnipotent and omniscient being can have no desire of having us seek His own ends because He can as easily bring about all His ends without us—and this appears of every and all objects. If we consider the case of excellency, from hence it follows that all excellency, when perceived, will be agreeable to perceiving being, and all evil disagreeable. But God, being omnipotent, must necessarily perfectly perceive all excellency and fully know what is contrary to it, and therefore all excellency is perfectly agreeable to His will, and all evil perfectly disagreeable. Therefore, He cannot will to do anything but what is excellent, but justice is all excellency.

So much evidence of the most perfect exactness of proportion, harmony, equity, and beauty in the mechanical laws of nature and other methods of providence, which belong to the course of nature, by which God shows his regard to harmony and fitness and beauty in what he does as the governor of the natural world, may strongly argue that he will maintain the most strict and perfect justice in proportion and fitness in what he does as the governor of the moral world.

If pardon and salvation are designed for the world, it is altogether meet that they should be proclaimed and promised. If they are not proclaimed and promised, there will be no sufficient assurance of them. Patience is not pardon, forbearance is not forgiveness, and if the divine patience administers some hope, yet the judgments of God upon the world will suggest as much anxiety and dread. And so, through fear of death and destruction, the self-conscious mind must be all its time subject to terror and bondage. If it is so hard for a sensible mind now, upon a public proclamation and promise to believe the forgiveness of sins, it would be much more difficult to believe it without any such security.

If pardon and salvation must be publicly proclaimed and promised to the guilty world, there will be an impediment or bar laid against it by the divine purity and justice. What sort of a Deity must that be that has an equal respect to good and evil? Universal rectitude requires that equity and equitable laws should be maintained and executed in the territories that are to be governed.

That there is vindictive justice in God seems evident

from the following:

1. From the excellency and perfection of His nature, by which He must hate all moral turpitude and all the workers of iniquity.

2. From His jealousy and concern for His own glory by which He will be displeased with all that is contrary thereto.

3. By the judgments which are continually executed in and upon the world for transgression, and sometimes by such special judgments that have been an evident retaliation or have marked out the sin in the punishment.

4. By the dictates of natural conscience that often trembles upon the commission of great enormities and expects that great transgressions should meet with some signal token of divine vengeance. When the barbarians saw the venomous animal hanging on Paul's hand, they concluded him to be some great criminal, whom though he had escaped from the rage of the sea, yet vengeance would not permit to live.

5. By the offense which men usually take at divine providence when it permits men to proceed and prosper in their notorious villanies.

6. By the early and universal practice of propitiatory sacrifices in the world. If they were at first instituted by God, then God would have an acknowledgment of our sin and His righteous displeasure in the atonement that was made him. If they were voluntarily taken up and practiced by men, there is an indication of mind and conscience that some deference must be paid to divine justice, and that to such a degree that they were sometimes ready in their ungoverned imaginations to sacrifice the fruit of their body for the sin of their soul.

The righteousness of God being this evident in itself and acknowledged by the world, that if man was to be pardoned by public edict and covenant, it was alto-

gether congruous thereto that there should be some
great valuable sacrifice slain and offered to God for the
sin of the world. It was meet that there should be a public demonstration of the holiness and purity of God
and of His hatred of sin so that the world may not be
tempted to abuse His goodness and presume upon His
mercy. It is meet that His dominion and authority
should be supported that had been so rejected by the
world; that His law, the rule of His government, should
be asserted and maintained; that His honor and glory,
after so much contempt and disgrace as the impious
world had cast upon Him, should be raised up and il-
lustrated; that the pardoning edict, being founded in
sacred blood, should be established and ratified, and
that, by a joint demonstration of justice and love, the
world may be driven from sin and drawn to repentance
and God. And here divine wisdom shines in reconcil-
ing righteousness and grace together, and accomplishing our salvation in the way and method of an eternal
redemption.

   This sacrifice should be valuable above all created
excellence and power. There is a world of most aggravated heinous offenses to be atoned for. It is an infinite
Majesty that has been offended. It is an infinite justice
that is to be propitiated. It is an infinite impunity, an
exemption from an endless punishment, and an advancement to an endless felicity that is to be procured.
All that intelligent creation can do for the Creator is
due to Him on its own account. Let all the intelligent
creatures take heed to themselves that they do not, by
their own fault, fall under the displeasure of God. His
majesty and justice may despise their interposition on
the behalf of an apostatized, sinful world.

   The Happiness of God: God stands in no need of
creatures, and is not profited by them. Neither can His

happiness be said to be added to by the creature; yet God has a real and proper delight in the excellency and happiness of His creatures. He has a real delight in the excellency and loveliness of the creature in His own image in the creature, as that is a manifestation, an expression, and shining forth of His own loveliness. God has a real delight in His own loveliness, and He also has a real delight in the shining forth and glorifying of it. As it is a fit and decent thing that God's glory should shine forth, so God delights in its shining forth. So God has a real delight in the spiritual loveliness of the saints, which delight is not a delight distinct from what He has in Himself, but is to be resolved into the delight He has in Himself. For He delights in His image in the creature as He delights in His own being glorified, or as He delights in it that His own glory shines forth. And so He has real, proper delight in the happiness of His creatures, which also is not distinct from the delight that He has in Himself, for it is to be resolved into the delight that He has in His own goodness.

As He delights in His own goodness, so He delights in the exercise of His goodness, and therefore He delights to make the creature happy, and delights to see Him made happy as He delights in exercising goodness or communicating happiness. This is no proper addition to the happiness of God, because it is that which He eternally and unalterably had. The happiness that God experiences when He beholds His own glory shining forth in His image in the creature, and when He beholds the creature made happy from the exercise of His goodness, does not increase, because those and all things are from eternity equally present with God. This delight in God cannot properly be said to be received from the creature because it consists only in a delight in giving to the creature. Neither will it hence follow that God is dependent on the creature for any of His joy, because it is His own act only that this delight is dependent on, and the creature is absolutely dependent on God for that excellency and happiness that God delights in. God cannot be said to be more happy because of the creature because He is infinitely happy in Himself. He is not dependent on the creature for anything, nor has He received any addition from the creature. And yet in one sense it can be truly said that God has more delight because of the loveliness and happiness of the creature, viz., as God would be less happy if He were less good, or if it were possible for Him to be hindered in exercising His own goodness, or to be hindered from glorifying Himself. God has no addition to His happiness when He exercises any act of holiness towards His creatures, and yet God has a real delight in the exercise of His own holiness, and would be less happy if He were less holy, or were capable of being hindered from any act of holiness.

Hence when the saints get to heaven they will have this to rejoice them, and add to their blessedness, that God has a real delight and joy in them, in their holiness and happiness.

Hence God's love to the saints is real and proper love, so that those have been to blame, who have represented much to the prejudice of religion, the love of God to creatures as if it were merely a purpose in God of acting as the creature does that has love.

Hence we learn how all God's love may be resolved into His love for and delight in Himself. His love to the creature is only His inclination to glorify Himself and communicate Himself, and His delight is in Himself glorified and in Himself communicated. There is His delight in the act and in the fruit. The act is the exercise of His own perfection, and the fruit is Himself expressed and communicated.

The Impassibility of God: There is no such thing truly as any pain, grief, or trouble in God. Hence it follows that there is no such thing as any real disappointment in God, of His being really crossed in His will, or things going contrary to His will, because according to the notion of will, to have one's will is agreeable and pleasing. For it is the notion of being pleased or suited to have things as we will them to be, and so, on the other hand, to have things contrary to one's will is disagreeable, troublesome, or uncomfortable. Job 23:13: "He is in one mind, and who can turn Him? And what His soul desireth, that He doth."

I suppose none will deny that, as to God's own actions, God decrees them, or purposes them beforehand. For none will be so absurd as to say that God acts without intentions, without designing to act, or that He forbears to act without intending to forbear. Also, whatsoever God intends or purposes, He intends and purposes from all eternity, and there are no new purposes or intentions in God. For if God sometimes begins to intend what He did not intend before, then two things will follow:

First, God is not omniscient. If God sometimes begins to design what He did not design before, it must of necessity be for want of knowledge, or for want of knowing things before as He knows them now, for want of having exactly the same views of things. If God begins to intend what He did not before intend, it must be because He now sees reasons to intend it that He did not see before, or that He has something newly brought to His understanding to influence Him.

Second, if God begins to intend or purpose things that He did not intend before, then God is certainly mutable, and then He must, in His own mind and will, be liable to succession and change; for wherever there are new things, there is succession and change.

Therefore, I shall take these two things for positions granted and supposed in this controversy: as to God's own actions and forbearings to act, He decrees and purposes them beforehand; and whatsoever God designs or purposes, He purposes from all eternity, and thus decrees from all eternity all His own actions and forbearings to act. Hence God decreed from all eternity to permit all the evil that ever He does permit, because God's permitting is God's forbearing to act or to prevent.

It can be made evident by reason that nothing can come to pass but what it is the will and pleasure of God should come to pass. This may be argued from the infinite happiness of God. For every being had rather things should go according to his will than not, because if he had not rather, then it is not his will. It is a contradiction to say he wills it and yet does not choose it, or had not rather it should be so than not. But if God had rather things should be according to His will than not, then if a thing falls out otherwise than He has willed, He meets with a cross, because, on this supposition, He had rather it should have been otherwise, and therefore He would have been better pleased if the thing had been otherwise. It is contrary to what He chooses, and therefore it is of necessity that He must be displeased. It is of necessity that every being should be pleased when a thing is as he chooses, or had rather it should be. It is a contradiction to suppose otherwise. For it is the very notion of being pleased to have things agreeable to one's pleasure. For the very same reason, every being is crossed, or it is unpleasing to him, when a thing is that he chose, and had rather should not have been. For it is the very notion of a thing's being cross or unpleasing to any that it is contrary to his pleasure.

But if God can meet with crosses and things un-

pleasing to Him, then He is not perfectly and unchangeably happy. For wherever there is any un-
pleasedness or unpleasantness, it must of necessity in a
degree diminish the happiness of the subject. Where
there is any cross to a being's choice, there is something contrary to happiness. Wherever there is any un-
pleasedness, there is something contrary to pleasure,
and which consequently diminishes pleasure. It is impossible anything should be plainer than this.

It may be argued from the infinite power and wisdom of God that nothing can come to pass but that it
must be agreeable to the will and pleasure of God that
it should come to pass. For, as was observed before, every being had rather things should be according to his
will than not. Therefore, if things are not according to
his will, it must be for want of power. It cannot be for
want of will. It must therefore be for want of sufficiency.
It must be either because he cannot have it so, or cannot have it so without some difficulty or some inconvenience. In other words, he lacks sufficiency to have
things as he wishes. But this cannot be the case with a
being of infinite power and wisdom. He can order all
things to be just as He wills, and He can order it with
perfect and infinite ease, or without the least difficulty
or inconvenience. Two things lie before him, both
equally within his power, either to order the matter to
be or not to order it to be, and both of them are equally
easy to Him. One is as little trouble to Him as the other,
since ease or trouble are perfectly equal. It is as easy for
Him to order it as not to order it. Therefore, His determination, whether it is ordering it or not ordering it,
must be a certain sign of His will in the case. If He orders it to be, this is a sign that His will is that it should
be. And if He does not order it to be, but allows it not to
be, that is as sure a sign that He wills that it should not
be. So that however the thing is, it is a sure sign that it

is the will of God that it should be as it is.

To this nothing can be objected, unless that it is not for lack of will or lack of power in God that things are not as He would have them, but because the nature of the subject will not allow for it. But how can this be the case when the nature of the subject itself is of God, and is wholly within His power, is altogether the fruit of His mere will? And cannot a God of infinite wisdom and infinite power cause the natures of things to be such, and order them so after they are caused, as to have things as He chooses, or without His will's being crossed, and things so coming to pass that He had rather have them otherwise?

If it will universally hold that none can have absolutely perfect and complete happiness at the same time that anything is otherwise than he desires at that time it should be, so thus, if it is true that he does not have absolute, perfect, infinite, and all possible happiness now, who does not now have all that he wills to have, then God, if anything is now otherwise than He wills to have it now, is not now absolutely, perfectly, and infinitely happy. If God is infinitely happy now, then everything is now as God would have it to be now; if everything, then those things that are contrary to His commands. If so, is it not ridiculous to say that things which are contrary to God's commands are yet in a sense agreeable to His will? Again, let it be considered, whether it is not certainly true that everyone who can with infinite ease have a thing done, and yet will not have it done, does not will it; that is, whether or not he who wills not to have a thing done properly wills not to have a thing done. For example: that Judas should be faithful to his Lord; is it not true that if God could, with infinite ease, have it done as He would, it is not proper to say that God would not have it be that Judas should be faithful to his Lord?

The Glory of God: God does not seek His own glory for any happiness He receives by it, as men are gratified in having their excellencies gazed at, admired, and extolled by others; but God seeks the display of His own glory as a thing excellent in itself. The display of the divine glory is that which is most excellent. It is good that glory should be displayed. The excellency of God's nature appears in that He loves and seeks whatever is excellent in itself. One way that the excellency of God's nature appears is in loving Himself, or loving His own excellency and infinite perfection. And as He loves His own perfection, so He loves the effulgence or shining forth of that perfection, or loves His own excellency in the expression and fruit of it. It is an excellent thing that that which is excellent should be expressed in proper act and fruit. Thus it is an excellent thing that infinite justice should shine forth and be expressed in infinitely just and righteous acts, and that infinite goodness should be expressed in infinitely good and gracious deeds.

God's glory, as it is spoken of in Scripture as the end of all God's works, is the emanation of that fullness of God that is from eternity in God, *ad extra*, and towards those creatures that are capable of being sensible and active objects of such an emanation. It consists in communicating Himself to those two faculties of the understanding and will, by which faculties it is that creatures are sensible and active objects or subjects of divine emanations and communications.

God communicates Himself to the understanding in the manifestation that is made of the divine excellency, and the understanding, idea, or view, which intelligent creatures have of it. He communicates His glory and fullness to the wills of sensible, willing, active beings in their rejoicing in the manifested glory of God, in their admiring it, in their loving God for it and being in all respects affected and disposed suitably to such glory, their exercising and expressing those affections and dispositions wherein consists their praising and glorifying God; in their being themselves holy and having the image of this glory in their hearts, and reflecting it as a jewel does the light of the sun, and partaking of God's brightness; and in their being happy in God, whereby they partake of God's fullness of happiness.

This twofold emanation or communication of the divine fullness *ad extra* is answerable to the twofold emanation or going forth of the Godhead *ad intra,* wherein the internal and essential glory and fullness of the Godhead consists, viz., the proceeding of the eternal Son of God, God's eternal idea and infinite understanding and wisdom, and the brightness of His glory, whereby His beauty and excellency appears to Him, and the proceeding of the Holy Spirit, or the eternal will, temper, disposition of the Deity, the infinite fullness of God's holiness, joy, and delight.

It is a proper and excellent thing for infinite glory to shine forth, and for the same reason it is proper that the shining forth of God's glory should be complete: that is, that all parts of His glory should shine forth, that every beauty should be proportionably effulgent, and that the beholder may have a proper notion of God. It is not proper that one glory should be exceedingly manifested and another not at all, for then the effulgence would not answer the reality. For the same reason, it is not proper that one should be manifested exceedingly and another but very little. It is highly proper that the effulgent glory of God should answer His real excellency; that the splendor should be answerable to the real and essential glory, for the same reason that it is proper and excellent for God to glorify Himself at all. Thus it is necessary that God's awful majesty, His authority and dreadful greatness, justice, and holiness, should be manifested. But this could not be unless sin and punishment had been decreed, so that the shining forth of God's glory would be very imperfect, both because these parts of divine glory would not shine forth as the others do, and also the glory of His goodness, love, and holiness would be faint without them—nay, they could scarcely shine forth at all. If it were not right that God should decree and permit and punish sin, there could be no manifestation of God's holiness in hatred of sin, or in showing any preference, in His providence, of godliness before it. There would be no manifestation of God's grace or true goodness if there was no sin to be pardoned, no misery to be saved from. However much happiness He bestowed, His goodness would not be so much prized and admired, and the sense of it not so great, as we have elsewhere shown. We little consider how much the sense of good is heightened by the sense of evil, both moral and natural. And as it is necessary that there should be evil—because the display of the glory of God could not but be imperfect and incomplete without it—so evil is necessary in order to the highest happiness of the creature, and the completeness of that communication of God, for which He made the world, because the creature's happiness consists in the knowledge of God, and in the sense of His love. And if the knowledge of Him is imperfect, the happiness of the creature must be proportionately imperfect, and the happiness of the creature would be imperfect upon another account also, for, as we have said, the sense of good is comparatively dull and flat without the knowledge of evil.

It may be asked why God would have the exercises of His perfections and the expressions of His glory known and published abroad. I answer, it was fitting that His attributes and perfections should be expressed. It was the will of God that they should be expressed and should shine forth. But if the expressions of His attributes are not known, they are not expressions; for the very being of the expression depends on the perception of created understandings. So much the more as the expression is known, so much the more it is.

The Goodness of God: It appears that there must be more than a unity in infinite and eternal essence. Otherwise the goodness of God can have no perfect exercise. To be perfectly good is to incline to and delight in making others happy in the same proportion as it is happy itself, that is, to delight as much in communicating happiness to another as enjoying it himself, and an inclination to communicate all his happiness. It appears that this is perfect goodness, because goodness and this delight are the same. But this delight is not perfect unless it is equal to the highest delight of that being, that is, unless his inclination to communicate happiness is equal to his inclination to be happy himself. Goodness is the exercise in communication of happiness. But if that communication is imperfect, that is, if it is not of all the happiness enjoyed by the being himself, the exercise of the goodness is imperfect inasmuch as the communication of happiness and the exercise of goodness is the same. But to no finite being can God either incline to communicate goodness so much as He inclines to be happy himself, for He cannot love a creature as much as He loves Himself, neither can He communicate all His goodness to a finite being. But no absolutely perfect being can be without absolutely perfect goodness, and no being can be perfectly happy which does not have the exercise of that which He sincerely inclines to exercise. Wherefore God must have a perfect exercise of His goodness, and therefore must have the fellowship of a person equal with Himself. No reasonable creature can be happy, we find, without society and communion, not only because it finds something in others that is not in himself, but because he delights to communicate himself to another. This cannot be because of our imperfection, but because we are made in the image of God. For the more perfect any creature is, the more strong is this inclination. So we may conclude that Jehovah's happiness consists in communion as well as the creature's.

The Grace of God

"And he shall bring forth the headstone thereof with shouting, crying, 'Grace, grace!' " Zechariah 4:7

The mercy of God is that attribute which we, the fallen, sinful race of Adam, stand in greatest need of, and God has been pleased, according to our needs, more gloriously to manifest this attribute than any other. The wonders of divine grace are the greatest of all wonders. The wonders of divine power and wisdom in the making of this great world are marvelous. Other wonders of His justice in punishing sin are wonderful; many wonderful things have happened since the creation of the world, but none like the wonders of grace. "Grace, grace!" is the sound that the gospel rings with. "Grace, grace!" will be that shout which will ring in heaven forever. What the angels sang at the birth of Christ, of God's good will towards men, is perhaps the highest theme that ever they entered upon.

In order to understand the words of our text, notice that the scope and design of the chapter is to comfort and encourage the children of Israel, returned out of their Babylonish captivity, in the building of Jerusalem and the temple. It seems that they were very much disheartened because of the opposition they met with in the work, and the lack of the external glory of the former temple before the captivity, so that the priests and the Levites, and the chief of the fathers, wept aloud as the rest shouted at the sight. This you may see in Ezra 3: 12: "But many of the priests and Levites, and chief of the fathers, who were ancient men, that had seen the first house, when the foundation of this house was laid before their eyes, wept with a loud voice, and many

26

shouted aloud for joy."

The prophets Haggai and Zechariah were sent on this occasion to comfort them under those discouragements by foretelling that the glories of the gospel should be displayed in this latter house, which should render the glories of it far beyond the glories of the former, notwithstanding it was so far exceeded in what is external. Haggai 2:3–9: " 'Who is left among you that saw this house in her first glory? And how do ye see it now? Is it not in your eyes in comparison of it as nothing? Yet now be strong, O Zerubbabel,' saith the Lord; 'and be strong, O Joshua, son of Josedech, the high priest; and be strong, all ye people of the land,' saith the Lord, 'and work; for I am with you,' saith the Lord of hosts, 'according to the word that I covenanted with you when ye came out of Egypt, so My Spirit remaineth among you; fear ye not.' For thus saith the Lord of hosts, 'Yet once, it is a little while, and I will shake the heavens, and the earth, and the sea, and the dry land. And I will shake all nations, and the desire of all nations shall come; and I will fill this house with glory,' saith the Lord of hosts. 'The silver is mine, and the gold is mine,' saith the Lord of hosts. 'The glory of this latter house shall be greater than of the former,' saith the Lord of hosts, 'and in this place will I give peace,' saith the Lord of hosts."

See also, in the third chapter of Zechariah and verse 8: "Hear now, O Joshua the high priest, thou and thy fellows that sit before thee; for they are men wondered at; for behold, I will bring forth My servant, the Branch." And the same subject is continued in this chapter, even the glorious grace of the gospel, which was to be manifested by Christ in this temple, particularly in our text, "and they shall bring forth the headstone with shouting, crying, 'Grace, grace unto it.' " The headstone is that which entirely crowns and finishes the whole work, signifying that the entire gospel dispensation was to be finished in mere grace.

This stone was to be brought with repeated shouting or rejoicings at the grace of God, signifying the admirableness and gloriousness of this grace.

DOCTRINE. The gospel dispensation is finished wholly and entirely in free and glorious grace. Glorious grace shines in every part of the great work of redemption: the foundation is laid in grace, the superstructure is reared in grace, and the whole is finished in glorious grace.

If Adam had stood and persevered in obedience, he would have been made happy by mere bounty and goodness; for God was not obliged to reward Adam for his perfect obedience any otherwise than by covenant, for Adam, by standing, would not have merited happiness. But this grace would not have been such as the grace of the gospel, for he would have been saved upon the account of what he himself did. But the salvation of the gospel is given altogether freely. Romans 11:6: "And if by grace, then it is no more works; otherwise grace is no more grace. But if it be of works, then it is no more grace; otherwise work is no more work."

That I may give you as full an explication of this doctrine as I can in a little space, I shall first show that free grace shines forth in the distinct parts of this wondrous work of redemption. Second, I shall speak a little of the gloriousness of this grace.

First, every part of this work was performed of mere grace. It was of free grace that God had any thoughts or designs of rescuing mankind after the fall. If there had not been an immense fountain of goodness in God, He would never have entertained any thoughts at all of ever redeeming us after our defection. Man was happy enough at first, and might have continued so to all eternity, if he would; he was not compelled to fall. If he

had not willfully and sinfully rebelled against God, he
would never have been driven forth like an unworthy
wretch as he was. But although God had been so overflowing in His bounty to him as to make him head over
the lower creation and ruler of all other creatures, and
had planted a garden on purpose for his delight, and
would have fixed him in an eternal happiness only on
the reasonable condition of his obeying the easy commands of his Maker, yet, notwithstanding all, he rebelled and turned from God to the devil, out of a
wicked ambition of being a god himself. He was not
content in that happy state that he was in as man, and
so rebelled against God's authority.

Now who but a God of boundless grace would not
have been provoked after this to leave man as he was, in
the miserable state into which he had brought himself
by his disobedience; resolving to help him no more,
leaving him to himself, and to the punishment he had
deserved; leaving him in the devil's hands where he
had thrown himself, not being contented in the arms
of his Creator. Who but one of boundless grace would
ever have entertained any thoughts of finding a way for
man's recovery?

God has no need of us or of our praises. He has
enough in Himself for Himself, and neither needs nor
desires any additions of happiness. If He did need the
worship of His creatures, He had thousands and
thousands of angels; and if He did not have enough,
He could create more. Or He could have glorified His
justice in man's eternal destruction and ruin, and
could have, with infinite ease, created other beings,
more perfect and glorious than man, eternally to sing
His praises.

But especially it was of rich and boundless grace
that He gave His only Son for our restoration. By our
fall, we are cast down so low into sin and misery, so

deeply plunged into a most miserable and sinful condition, that it may truly be said, although all things are infinitely easy to God with respect to His omnipotency, yet with respect God's holiness and justice, God Himself could not redeem us without a great deal of cost, no, not without infinite costs; that is, not without the presence of that which is of infinite worth and value, even the blood of His Son, and properly speaking, the blood of God, in the form of a divine person.

This was absolutely necessary in order to our redemption, because there was no other way to satisfying God's justice. When we were alien, it came to this: either we must die eternally or the Son of God must spill His blood; either we or God's own Son must suffer God's wrath, one of the two; either miserable worms of the dust that had deserved it, or the glorious, amiable, beautiful, and innocent Son of God. The fall of man brought it to this; it must be determined one way or the other and it was determined by the strangely free and boundless grace of God that His own Son should die so that the offending worms might be freed and set at liberty from their punishment, and that justice might make them happy. Here is grace indeed; well may we shout, "Grace, grace!" at this.

The heathens used to reckon that an only son slain in sacrifice was the greatest gift that could be offered to the gods. It was what they used sometimes to offer in times of great distress, and in some parts of the world it is constantly at this day performed. But we have a stranger thing than that declared to us in the gospel, not that men sacrificed their only sons to God, but that God gave His only Son to be slain as a sacrifice for man. God once commanded Abraham to offer his only son to Him, and perhaps the faith and love of Abraham may be looked upon as wonderful, that he was willing to perform it. There are few who would do it in these days.

But if you wonder at that, how wonderful is it that, instead of Abraham's offering his only son to God, God should give His only Son to be offered for Abraham, and for every child of Abraham. Certainly, you will acknowledge this to be a wonder not to be paralleled.

And besides, God did not do this for friends, but for enemies and haters of Him. He did not do it for loyal subjects, but for rebels. He did not do it for those who were His children, but for the children of the devil. He did not do it for those who were excellent, but for those who were more hateful than toads or vipers. He did not do it for those who could in any way be profitable or advantageous to Him, but for those who were so weak that, instead of profiting God, they were not able in the least to help themselves.

God has given even fallen man such a gift that He has left nothing for man to do that he may be happy but to receive what is given to him. Though he has sinned, yet God requires no amends to be made by him. He requires of him no restoration; if they will receive His Son from Him, He requires neither money nor price. Man is to do no penance in order to be forgiven. What God offers, He offers freely. God offers man eternal happiness upon far more gracious terms since he is fallen than before. Before, he had to do something himself for his happiness: he was to obey the law. But since he is fallen, God offers to save him for nothing, only if he will receive salvation as it is offered, that is, freely through Christ and by faith in Him.

It was of mere grace that the Son was so freely willing to undertake our salvation. How cheerfully, yea, how joyfully did He undertake it, although He Himself was the very person who was to suffer for man. Though He Himself was to bear his sin and be made sin for him, yet how cheerfully does He speak in Ps. 40:7–8: "Lo, I come; in the volume of the book it is written of me, 'I delight to do Thy will, O God.' " He says in Proverbs 8:31 that His "delights were with the sons of men," for so did He love them that it seems He Himself was willing to die in their place rather than that they should be miserable. He freely undertook this out of mere love and pity, for He never was and never will be repaid by them for His blood.

The application of the redemption of the gospel by the Holy Spirit is of mere grace. Although God the Father has provided a Savior for us, and Christ has come and died, and there is nothing wanting but our willing and hearty reception of Christ, yet we shall eternally perish if God is not gracious to us, and don't make application of Christ's benefits to our souls. We are dependent on free grace even for ability to lay hold of Christ already offered, so entirely is the gospel dispensation of mere grace. Ephesians 2:8–10: "For by grace are ye saved through faith, and that not of yourselves: it is the gift of God." That is, we shall be saved freely and for nothing if we will but accept Christ, but we are not able to do that of ourselves. It is the free gift of God, "not of works, lest any man should boast, for we are His workmanship, created in Christ Jesus unto good works, which God hath before ordained that we should walk in them."

Second, I shall now briefly speak to the gloriousness of this grace. As the grace of the gospel is altogether free, so it is glorious; the angels stoop down, with eyes full of wonder and joy, to look into and shout for gladness and admiration at the sight of it. How did the multitudes of heavenly hosts shout at the birth of Christ, crying, "Glory to God in the highest; on earth peace and good will towards men!" Well may the topstone of this house be brought forth with shouting, crying, "Grace, grace!" to it.

All the attributes of God illustriously shine forth in the face of Jesus Christ. His wisdom in so contriving, His power in conquering death and the devil and the hard and rocky hearts of depraved men, His justice in punishing the sins of men upon His own dear Son rather than let it go unpunished; but more especially in His grace, that sweet attribute, He has magnified His mercy above all His names.

The grace of God exhibited in the gospel is glorious, first, because of the greatness of it. Grace surprisingly heightens every circumstance of the gospel. Let us look on whatever part we will, we shall see enough to fill us and all the angels in heaven with admiration forever. If we consider it as the grace of God the Father, and consider His greatness, His holiness, His power and justice, His immensity and eternity; if we diligently consider how great a Being He is, who took such pity and compassion on mankind, it is enough to astonish us. Or, if we consider ourselves, on whom this great God has bestowed this grace, we are nothing but worms, yea, less than worms before God; and not only so, but sinful worms, worms swollen with enmity against God. If we consider Him by whom we receive grace, the Son of God who made heaven and, by His almighty power, is equal with the Father; if we consider the greatness of what He did, dying most ignominiously and painfully in our nature—it all infinitely heightens the grace of the gospel.

The grace of God exhibited in the gospel is glorious, second, because of the glorious fruit of it. No less than salvation and eternal glory are the fruits of this grace of the gospel; adoption, union with Christ, communion with God, the indwelling of the Holy Ghost, the heavenly happiness, the pleasure of the eternal paradise, the new Jerusalem, the glorious and triumphant resurrection of the body, and an everlasting reign with

Christ in the height of glory, and pleasure and happiness; no less than these things are the effects of this marvelous grace.

What a vast difference is there between a poor, miserable sinner, full of sin and condemned to hellfire, and a saint shining forth in robes of glory and crowned with a crown of victory and triumph; but no less difference than this is made in the same man by the grace of God in Christ.

Application

Hence we learn how they dishonor God and the gospel who depend on anything else but mere grace. The gospel is far the most glorious manifestation of God's glory that ever was made to man, and the glory of the gospel is free grace and mere mercy. Now those who will not depend on this free grace do what they can to deprive the gospel of this glory, and sully the glory of God therein shining forth. They take away the praise, glory, and honor that is due to God by His free grace and mercy to men, and set up themselves as the objects of it, as if their salvation at least partly was owing to what they have done.

This must be very provoking and highly affronting to God, for miserable sinners, after they have fallen into such a miserable estate that it is impossible they should be saved by any other means than pure grace, and God is so gloriously rich in His goodness as to offer this free grace unto them out of pity to them—how provoking must it be to God for these miserable, helpless wretches to attribute any of their salvation to themselves!

It is not an opportunity to buy and procure our own salvation that God offers, but an opportunity to lay hold on that salvation which is already bought and procured for us. Neither are we able to do this of ourselves; it is the gift of God.

There are some who hope to be saved in quite another way than ever the gospel proposed, that is, by their own righteousness, by being so good and doing so well that God shall take their goodness as sufficient to counterbalance their sin that they have committed. And thereby they make their own goodness of equal value with Christ's blood. This conceit is very apt to creep into the proud heart of man.

Some openly profess to be able to merit salvation, such as papists. Others hold that they are able to prepare and fit themselves for salvation already merited, or at least are able to do something towards it of themselves. And it is to be feared that many who don't openly profess either their own righteousness or their own strength very much depend upon both. By this doctrine, how much they dishonor the free grace of the gospel!

Let all be exhorted to accept the grace of the gospel. One would think that there should be no need of such exhortations as this, but, alas, such is the dreadful wickedness and the horrible ingratitude of man's heart that he needs an abundance of persuading and entreating to accept God's kindness when offered to him. We should count it horrible ingratitude in a poor, necessitous creature to refuse our help and kindness when we, out of mere pity to him, offer to relieve and help him. If you should see a man in extreme distress, and in a perishing necessity of help and relief, and you should lay out yourself with much labor and cost out of compassion to him, that he might be relieved, how would you take it of him if he should proudly and spitefully refuse it and snuff at it instead of thanking you for it? Would you not look upon it as a very ungrateful, unreasonable, base thing? And why has not God a thousand times

more cause to look upon you as base and ungrateful if
you refuse His glorious grace in the gospel that He offers you? When God saw mankind in a most necessitous
condition, in the greatest and most extreme distress,
being exposed to hellfire and eternal death, from
which it was impossible he should ever deliver himself,
or that ever he should be delivered by any other means,
He took pity on him, and brought him from the jaws of
destruction by His own blood. Now what great ingratitude is it for them to refuse such grace as this!

But so it is. Multitudes will not accept a free gift at
the hands of the King of the world. They have the daring, horrible presumption to refuse a kindness offered
by God Himself, and not to accept a gift at the hands of
Jehovah, nor His own Son, who is equal with Himself.
Yea, they'll not accept Him though He dies for them,
yea, though He dies a most tormenting death, though
He dies that they may be delivered from hell, and that
they may have heaven. They'll not accept this gift
though they are in such necessity of it that they must be
miserable forever without it. Yea, although God the
Father invites and importunes them, they'll not accept
it; though the Son of God Himself knocks and calls at
their door till His head is wet with the dew and His
locks with the drops of the night, arguing and plead-
ing with them to accept Him for their own sakes,
though He makes so many glorious promises, though
He holds forth so many precious benefits to tempt
them to happiness, perhaps for many years together, yet
they obstinately refuse all. Was ever such ingratitude
heard of, or can greater be conceived of?

What would you have God do for you that you may
accept it? Is the gift that He offers so small that you
think it too little for you to accept ? God offers you His
Son, and what could God offer more? Yea, we may say
God Himself has no greater gift to offer. Did not the

Son of God do enough for you? Is that why you won't
accept Him? Did He die? What more could He do? Yea,
we may say that the Son of God could not do a greater
thing for man. Do you refuse because you want to be invited and wooed? You may hear Him, from day to day,
inviting you if you will but hearken. Or is it because you
don't stand in need of God's grace? You need it so
much that you must either receive it or be damned to
all eternity. And what greater need could there possibly
be?

Alas, miserable creatures that we are, instead of the
gift of God offered in the gospel's not being great
enough for us, we are not worthy of anything at all. We
are less than the least of all God's mercies. Instead of
deserving the dying Son of God, we are not worthy of
the least crumb of bread, the least drop of water, or the
least ray of light. Instead of Christ's not having done
enough for us by dying in such pain and ignominy, we
are not worthy that He should so much as look on us
instead of shedding His blood. We are not worthy that
Christ should once make an offer of the least benefit
instead of His so long urging us to be eternally happy.

Whoever continues to refuse Christ will find hereafter that, instead of his having no need of Him, the
least drop of His blood would have been worth more to
him than all the world. Therefore, let none be so ungrateful to God, and so unwise for themselves, as to
refuse the glorious grace of the gospel.

Let those who have been made partakers of this free
and glorious grace of God spend their lives much in
praises and hallelujahs to God for the wonders of His
mercy in their redemption. To you, O redeemed of the
Lord, this doctrine most directly applies itself. You are
those who have been made partakers of all this glorious
grace of which you have now heard. 'Tis you whom God
entertained thoughts of restoring after your miserable

fall into dreadful depravity and corruption, and into danger of the dreadful misery that unavoidably follows upon it. 'Tis for you in particular that God gave His Son, yea, His only Son, and sent Him into the world. 'Tis for you that the Son of God so freely gave Himself. 'Tis for you that He was born, died, rose again, ascended, and intercedes. 'Tis to you that there the free application of the fruit of these things is made. All this is done perfectly and altogether freely, without any of your desert, without any of your righteousness or strength; wherefore, let your life be spent in praises to God. When you praise Him in prayer, let it not be with coldness and indifference; when you praise Him in your closet, let your whole soul be active therein; when you praise Him in singing, don't barely make a noise, without any stirring of affection in the heart, without any internal melody. Surely you have reason to shout and cry, "Grace, grace be the topstone of the temple!" Certainly, you don't lack mercy and bounty to praise God; you only lack a heart and lively affections to praise Him with.

Surely, if the angels are so astonished at God's mercy to you, and even shout with joy and admiration at the sight of God's grace to you, you yourself, on whom this grace is bestowed, have much more reason to shout.

Consider that great part of your happiness in heaven, to all eternity, will consist in praising God for His free and glorious grace in redeeming you. And if you would spend more time about it on earth, you would find this world would be much more of a heaven to you than it is. Therefore, do nothing while you live but speak and think and live God's praises.

The Sovereignty of God

"Be still, and know that I am God." Psalm 46:10

This psalm seems to be a song of the church in a time of great revolutions and desolations in the world. Therefore the church glories in God as her refuge, strength, and present help, even in times of the greatest troubles and overturnings. Verses 1–3: "God is our refuge and strength, a very present help in trouble. Therefore will we not fear, though the earth be removed, and though the mountains be carried into the midst of the sea; though the waters thereof roar and be troubled, though the mountains shake with the swelling thereof." The church makes her boast of God not only as being her help—by defending her from the desolations and calamities in which the rest of the world were involved—but also by supplying her as a never-failing river with refreshment, comfort, and joy in the times of public calamities. See verses 4–5: "There is a river, the streams whereof shall make glad the city of God, the holy place of the tabernacles of the Most High. God is in the midst of her; she shall not be moved. God shall help her, and that right early."

The 6th and 8th verses set forth the terrible changes and calamities which were in the world: "The heathen raged, the kingdoms were moved. He uttered His voice, the earth melted. Come, behold the works of God, what desolations He hath made in the earth." The verse preceding the text elegantly sets forth the manner in which God delivers the church from these calamities, and especially from the desolations of war and the rage of their enemies: "He maketh wars to cease unto the end of the earth; He breaketh the bow, and cutteth the

spear in sunder; He burneth the chariot in the fire." In
other words, He makes wars to cease when they are
against His people. He breaks the bow when it is bent
against His saints.

Then follow the words of the text: "Be still, and
know that I am God." The great works of God, wherein
His sovereignty appeared, had been described in the
foregoing verses. In the awful desolations that He
made, and by delivering His people by terrible things,
He showed his greatness and dominion. Herein He
manifested His power and sovereignty, and so commands all to be still and know that He is God. For, says
He, "I will be exalted among the heathen; I will be exalted in the earth."

In the words may be observed:

A duty described: to be still before God, and under
the dispensations of His providence. This implies that
we must be still as to words, not speaking against the
sovereign dispensations of Providence, or complaining
of them; not darkening counsel by words without
knowledge, or justifying ourselves and speaking great
swelling words of vanity. We must be still as to actions
and outward behavior, so as not to oppose God in His
dispensations; and as to the inward frame of our hearts,
cultivating a calm and quiet submission of soul to the
sovereign pleasure of God, whatever it is.

The ground of this duty: the divinity of God. His
being God is a sufficient reason why we should be still
before Him, in no wise murmuring, objecting, or
opposing, but calmly and humbly submitting to Him.

How we must fulfill this duty of being still before
God: with a sense of His divinity as seeing the ground
of this duty, in that we know Him to be God. Our submission is to be such as becomes rational creatures.
God does not require us to submit contrary to reason,
but to submit as seeing the reason and ground of sub-

mission. Hence, the bare consideration that God is God may well be sufficient to still all objections and opposition against the divine sovereign dispensations.)
This may appear by the following things:
1. In that He is God, He is an absolutely and infinitely perfect Being; and it is impossible that He should do amiss. As He is eternal, and does not receive His existence from any other, He cannot be limited in His being, or any attribute, to any certain, determinate quantity. If anything has bounds fixed to it, there must be some cause or reason why those bounds are fixed just where they are. Whence it will follow, that every limited thing must have some cause. And therefore that being which has no cause must be unlimited.

It is most evident by the works of God that His understanding and power are infinite. For He who has made all things out of nothing, and upholds, governs, and manages all things every moment in all ages, without growing weary, must be of infinite power. He must also be of infinite knowledge; for if He made all things, and upholds and governs all things continually, it will follow that He knows and perfectly sees all things, great and small, in heaven and earth, continually at one view, which cannot be without infinite understanding.

Being thus infinite in understanding and power, He must also be perfectly holy; for unholiness always argues some defect or some blindness. Where there is no darkness or delusion, there can be no unholiness. It is impossible that wickedness should consist with infinite light. God, being infinite in power and knowledge, must be self-sufficient and all-sufficient. Therefore it is impossible that He should be under any temptation to do anything amiss; for He can have no end in doing it. When any are tempted to do amiss, it is for selfish ends. But how can an all-sufficient Being, who lacks nothing, be tempted to do evil for selfish ends? So God is essen-

tially holy, and nothing is more impossible than that
God should do amiss.

2. As He is God, He is so great that He is infinitely
above all comprehension. And therefore it is unreasonable in us to quarrel with His dispensations, because they are mysterious. If He were a Being that we
could comprehend, He would not be God. It would be
unreasonable to suppose any other than that there
should be many things in the nature of God, and in His
works and government, which to us are mysterious, and
which we never can fully find out.

What are we? And what do we make of ourselves
when we expect that God and His ways should be upon
a level with our understandings? We are infinitely unequal to any such thing as comprehending God. We
may less unreasonably expect that a nutshell should
contain the ocean. Job 11:7–9: "Canst thou by searching
find out God? Canst thou find out the Almighty unto
perfection? It is as high as heaven, what canst thou do?
Deeper than hell, what canst thou know? The measure
thereof is longer than the earth, and broader than the
sea." If we were sensible of the distance between God
and us, we would see the reasonableness of that inter-
rogation of the apostle in Romans 9:20: "Who art thou,
O man, that repliest against God?"

If we find fault with God's government, we virtually
suppose ourselves fit to be God's counselors; whereas it
becomes us rather, with great humility and adoration,
to cry out with the apostle in Romans 11:33–36: "O the
depth of the riches, both of the wisdom and knowledge
of God! How unsearchable are His judgments, and His
ways past finding out! For who hath known the mind of
the Lord? Or who hath been His counselor? Or who
hath first given to Him and it shall be recompensed
unto Him again? For of Him, and through Him, and to
Him are all things, to whom be glory forever." If little

children should rise up and find fault with the supreme legislature of a nation, or quarrel with the mysterious administrations of the sovereign, would it not be looked upon that they meddled with things too high for them? And what are we but babes? Our understandings are infinitely less than those of babes in comparison with the wisdom of God. It becomes us therefore to be sensible of it, and to behave ourselves accordingly. Psalm 131:1–2: "Lord, my heart is not haughty, nor mine eyes lofty; neither do I exercise myself in great matters, or in things too high for me. Surely I have behaved and quieted myself as a child." This consideration alone of the infinite distance between God and us, and between God's understanding and ours, should be enough to still and quiet us concerning all that God does, however mysterious and unintelligible to us. Nor have we any right to expect that God should particularly explain to us the reason for His dispensations. It is fitting that God should not give any account of His matters to us worms of the dust, so that we may be sensible of our distance from Him, and adore and submit to Him in humble reverence.

Therefore we find that when Job was so full of difficulty about the divine dispensations, God did not answer him by particularly explaining the reasons for His mysterious providence, but by showing him what a poor worm, what a nothing he was, and how much He Himself was above him. This more became God than it would have done to enter into a particular debate with Job, or to unfold the mysterious difficulties. It became Job to submit to God in those things that he could not understand, and to this the reply tended to bring him. It is fitting that God should dwell in thick darkness, or in light to which no man can approach, which no man has seen nor can see. No wonder that a God of infinite glory shines with a brightness too strong and mighty for mortal eyes; for the angels themselves, those mighty spirits, are represented as covering their faces in this light (Isaiah 6).

3. As He is God, all things are His own, and He has a right to dispose of them according to His own pleasure. All things in this lower world are His. Job 41:11: "Whatsoever is under the whole heaven is mine." Yea, the whole universe is God's. Deuteronomy 10:14: "Behold the heaven, and the heaven of heavens is the Lord's; the earth also, with all that is therein." All things are His because all things are from Him; they are wholly from Him, and from Him alone. Those things which are made by men are not wholly from them. When a man builds a house, it is not wholly from him. Nothing of which the house is made has its being from him. But all creatures are wholly and entirely the fruits of God's power, and therefore it is fitting that they should be subject to and for His pleasure (Proverbs 16:4). And as all things are from God, so they are upheld in being by Him, and would sink into nothing in a moment if He did not uphold them. All things are to him. Romans 11:36: "For by Him, and through Him, and to him are all things." Colossians 1:16–17: "For by Him were all things created that are in heaven, and that are in earth, visible and invisible, whether they be thrones or dominions, principalities or powers; all things were created by Him and for Him. And He is before all things, and by Him all things consist." All mankind is His: their lives, breath, and being, "for in Him we live, and move, and have our being." Our souls and capacities are from Him. Ezekiel 18:4: "All souls are Mine; as the soul of the father, so also the soul of the son is Mine."

4. In that He is God, He is worthy to be sovereign over all things. Sometimes men are the owners of more than they are worthy of. But God is not only the owner

of the whole world, as all is from and dependent on Him, but such is His perfection, the excellency and dignity of His nature, that He is worthy of sovereignty over all. No man ought in the temper of his mind to be opposed to God's exercising the sovereignty of the universe, as if He were not worthy of it; for to be the absolute sovereign of the universe is not a glory or dignity too great for Him. All things in heaven and earth, angels and men, are nothing in comparison with Him. All are as the drop of the bucket, and as the light dust of the balance. It is therefore fitting that everything should be in His hands, to be disposed of according to His pleasure. His will and pleasure are of infinitely greater importance than the will of creatures. It is fitting that His will should take place, though contrary to the will of all other beings; that He should make Himself His own end, and order all things for Himself. God is possessed of such perfections and excellencies as to qualify Him to be the absolute sovereign of the world. Certainly it is more fitting that all things be under the guidance of a perfect, unerring wisdom than that they should be left to themselves to fall in confusion, or be brought to pass by blind causes. Yea, it is not fitting that any affairs within the government of God should be left without the direction of His wise providence, least of all things of the greatest importance.

It is absurd to suppose that God is obliged to keep every creature from sinning and exposing himself to an adequate punishment. For if so, then it will follow that there can be no such thing as a moral government of God over reasonable creatures. And it would be an absurdity for God to give commands, for He Himself would be the party bound to see to the performance, and there could be no use of promises or threatenings. But if God may leave a creature to sin and to expose himself to punishment, then it is much more fitting and better that the matter should be ordered by wisdom who should justly lie exposed by sin to punishment and who not; than that it be left to come to pass by confused chance. It is unworthy of the Governor of the world to leave things to chance; it belongs to Him to govern all things by wisdom. And as God has wisdom to qualify Him to be sovereign, so He has power also to enable Him to execute the determinations of wisdom. He is essentially and invariably holy and righteous, and infinitely good, whereby He is qualified to govern the world in the best manner. Therefore, when He acts as sovereign of the world, it is fitting that we should be still and willingly submit, and in no wise oppose His having the glory of His sovereignty. Rather, in a sense of His worthiness, we should cheerfully ascribe it to Him and say, "Thine is the kingdom and the power and the glory forever," and say with those in Revelation 5:13: "Blessing, and honor, and glory, and power, be to Him that sitteth upon the throne."

5. In that He is God, He will be sovereign, and will act as such. He sits on the throne of His sovereignty, and His kingdom "ruleth over all." He will be exalted in His sovereign power and dominion, as He himself declares: "I will be exalted among the heathen. I will be exalted in the earth." He will have all men to know that He is most high over all the earth. He does according to His will in the armies of heaven and among the inhabitants of the earth, and none can stay His hand. There is no such thing as frustrating, baffling, or undermining His designs, for He is great in counsel and wonderful in working. His counsel shall stand, and He will do all his pleasure. There is no wisdom, nor understanding, nor counsel against the Lord. Whatsoever God does, it shall be forever. Nothing shall be put to it, nor anything taken from it. He will work, and who shall stop it? He is able to dash in pieces the enemy. If

men join hand in hand against Him to hinder or oppose His designs, He breaks the bow. He cuts the spear asunder, and burns the chariot in the fire. He kills and He makes alive. He brings down and raises up just as He pleases. Isaiah 45:6–7: "That they may know from the rising of the sun, and from the west, that there is none besides Me. I am the Lord, and there is none else. I form the light and create darkness. I make peace and create evil. I the Lord do all these things."

Great men, rich men, and wise men cannot hinder God from doing His pleasure. He leads counselors away spoiled. He does not accept the persons of princes, nor does He regard the rich more than the poor. There are many devices in a man's heart, but the counsel of the Lord shall stand, and the thoughts of His heart to all generations. When He gives quietness, who can make trouble? When He hides His face, who can behold Him? He breaks down, and it cannot be built up again. He shuts up a man, and there can be no opening. When He purposes, who shall disannul it? And when His hand is stretched out, who shall turn it back?

So there is no hindering God from being sovereign, and acting as such. "He hath mercy on whom He will have mercy, and whom He will He hardeneth." He has the keys of hell and of death. He opens and no man shuts. He shuts and no man opens. This may show us the folly of opposing ourselves against the sovereign dispensations of God, and how much more wisely they act who quietly and sweetly submit to His sovereign will.

6. In that He is God, He is able to avenge Himself on those who oppose His sovereignty. He is wise of heart and mighty in strength. Who has hardened himself against God and prospered? He who will contend with God must answer it. And what a poor creature is man to fight against God! Is he able to make his part good with

Him? Whoever of God's enemies deal proudly, He will show that He is above them. They will be but as the chaff before the whirlwind, and shall be as the fat of lambs. They shall be consumed into smoke. "Who would set the briers and thorns against Him in battle? He would go through them, He would burn them together" (Isaiah 27:4).

Application

A manifold improvement might be made of this doctrine, which a little reflection may suggest to each of us. But the application which I shall at this time make of it shall be only in a use of reproof to such as oppose the sovereignty of God in the disposals of His grace. This doctrine shows the unreasonableness, and dreadful wickedness, of your refusing heartily to own the sovereignty of God in this matter. It shows that you do not know that God is God. If you knew this, you would be inwardly still and quiet; you would humbly and calmly lie in the dust before a sovereign God, and would see sufficient reason for it.

In objecting and quarreling about the righteousness of God's laws and threatenings, and His sovereign dispensations towards you and others, you oppose His divinity. You show your ignorance of His divine greatness and excellency, and that you cannot bear that He should have divine honor. It is from low, mean thoughts of God that in your minds you oppose His sovereignty, that you are not sensible how dangerous your conduct is; and what an audacious thing it is for such a creature as man to strive with his Maker!

What poor creatures are you that you should set up yourselves as judges over the Most High; that you should take it upon yourself to call God to an account;

that you should say to the great Jehovah, "What are you doing?" and that you should pass sentence against Him! If you know that He is God, you would not act in this manner. But this knowledge would be sufficient to still and calm you concerning all God's dispensations, and you would say with Eli, in 1 Samuel 3:18, "It is the Lord, let Him do what seemeth good in His sight."

But here I shall be more particular in several things:

1. It is from mean thoughts of God that you are not convinced that you have, by your sins, deserved His eternal wrath and curse. If you had any proper sense of the infinite majesty, greatness, and holiness of God, you would see that to be cast into the lake of fire and brimstone, and there to have no rest day nor night, is not a punishment more than equal to the demerit of sin. You would not have so good a thought of yourselves; you would not be so clean and pure in your own eyes; you would see the vile, unworthy, hell-deserving creatures you are. If you did not have little thoughts of God, and were to consider how you have set yourselves against Him—how you have slighted Him, His commandments and threatenings, and despised His goodness and mercy, how often you have disobeyed, how obstinate you have been, how your whole lives have been filled up with sin against God—you would not wonder that God threatens to destroy you forever, but would wonder that He has not actually done it before now.

If you did not have mean thoughts of God, you would not find fault with Him for not setting His love on you, who never exercised any love to Him. You would not think it unjust of God not to seek your interest and eternal welfare, who never would be persuaded at all to seek His glory. You would not think it unjust in Him to slight and disregard you, who have so often and so long made light of God. If you did not have low thoughts of God, you never would think Him obliged to bestow eternal salvation upon you, who have never been truly thankful for one mercy which you have already received from Him. What do you think of yourselves? What great ideas have you of yourselves? And what thoughts have you of God, that you think He is obliged to do so much for you, though you treat Him ever so ungratefully for the kindness which He has already bestowed upon you all the days of your lives? It must be from little thoughts of God that you think it unjust of Him not to regard you when you call upon Him, when He has earnestly called to you so long and so often, and you would not be persuaded to hearken to Him. What thoughts have you of God that you think He is more obliged to hear what you say to Him than you are to regard what He says to you?

It is from diminutive thoughts of God that you think He is obliged to show mercy to you when you seek it, though you have been for a long time willfully sinning against Him, provoking Him to anger, and presuming that He would show you mercy when you should seek it. What kind of thoughts have you of God that you think He is obliged, as it were, to yield Himself up to be abused by men so that, when they are done, His mercy and pardoning grace shall not be in His own power, but He must be obliged to dispense them at their call?

2. It is from little thoughts of God that you quarrel against His justice in the condemnation of sinners from the doctrine of original sin. It must be because you do not know Him to be God, and will not allow Him to be sovereign. It is for want of a sense how much God is above you that those things in Him which are above your comprehension are such difficulties and stumbling blocks to you. It is for want of a sense of how much the wisdom and understanding of God are above yours, and what poor, shortsighted, blind creatures you are in comparison with Him. If you were sensible what God is, you would see it most reasonable to expect that

His ways should be far above the reason of man, and
that He dwells in light which no man can approach
unto, which no man has seen nor can see. If men were
sensible of how excellent and perfect a Being He is,
they would not be so apt to be jealous of Him and to
suspect Him in things which lie beyond their understandings. It would be no difficulty with them to trust
God out of sight. What horrid arrogance in worms of
the dust, that they should think they have wisdom
enough to examine and determine concerning what
God does, and to pass sentence on it as unjust! If you
were sensible of how great and glorious a being God is,
it would not be such a difficulty with you to allow Him
the dignity of such absolute sovereignty, as that He
should order as he pleases, whether every single man
should stand for himself, or whether a common father
should stand for all.

3. It is from mean thoughts of God that you trust in
your own righteousness, and think that God ought to
respect you for it. If you knew how great a Being He is,
if you saw that He is God indeed, you would see how
unworthy, how miserable a present it is to be offered to
such a Being. It is because you are blind, and do not
know not what a Being He is with whom you have to do,
that you make so much of your own righteousness. If
you had your eyes open to see that He is God indeed,
you would wonder how you could think to commend
yourselves to so great a Being by your gifts, by such poor
affections, such broken prayers, wherein is so much
hypocrisy and so much selfishness. If you did not have
very mean thoughts of God, you would wonder that ever
you could think of purchasing the favor and love of so
great a God by your services. You would see that it would
be unworthy of God to bestow such a mercy upon you—
peace with Him, His everlasting love, and the enjoyment of Himself—for such a price as you have to offer;

and that He would exceedingly dishonor Himself in so doing. If you saw what God is, you would exclaim, as Job did in Job 42:5–6, "Now mine eye seeth Thee; wherefore I abhor myself, and repent in dust and ashes." And as Isaiah did in Isaiah 6:5, "Woe is me, for I am undone, because I am a man of unclean lips; for mine eyes have seen the King, the Lord of hosts."

4. It is from mean thoughts of God that you contend with Him because He bestows grace on some and not on others. God has mercy on whom He will have mercy. He takes one and leaves another, of those who are in like circumstances; as it is said of Jacob and Esau, while they were not yet born, and had done neither good nor evil (Romans 9:10–13). With this sinners often quarrel. But they who upon this ground quarrel with God suppose Him to be bound to bestow His grace on sinners. (For if He is bound to none, then He may make His choice and bestow it on whom He pleases.) And His bestowing it on some brings no obligation on Him to bestow it on others. Has God no right to His own grace? Is it not at His own disposal? And is God incapable of making a gift or present of it to any man? For a person cannot make a present of that which is not His own or in his own right. It is impossible to give a debt.

What a low thought of God this argues! Consider what it is you would make of God. Must He be so tied up that He cannot use His own pleasure in bestowing His own gifts? Is He obliged to bestow them on one because it is His pleasure to bestow them on another? Is not God worthy to have the same right to dispose of His gifts as a man has of his money? Or is it because God is not so great, and therefore should be more subject, more under bounds, than men? Is not God worthy to have as absolute a propriety in His goods as man has in his? At this rate, God cannot make a present of anything. He has nothing of his own to bestow. If He has a mind to show a peculiar favor to some, to lay some under special obligations, He cannot do it on the supposition that His favor is not at His own disposal! The truth is, men have low thoughts of God or else they would willingly ascribe sovereignty to Him in this matter. Matthew 20:15: "Is it not lawful for Me to do what I will with Mine own? Is thine eye evil because I am good?"

God is pleased to show mercy to His enemies according to His own sovereign pleasure. And surely it is fitting that He should. How unreasonable is it to think that God stands bound to His enemies! Therefore consider what you do in quarreling with God and opposing His sovereignty. Consider with whom it is you contend. Let all who are sensible of their misery, and afraid of the wrath of God, consider these things. Those of you who have been long seeking salvation, but are in great terrors through fear that God will destroy you, consider what you have heard, be still, and know that he is God. When God seems to turn a deaf ear to your cries; when He seems to frown upon you; when He shows mercy to others, your equals, or those who are worse, and who have been seeking a less time than you—be still. Consider who He is who disposes and orders these things. You shall consider it. You shall know it. He will make all men to know that He is God. You shall either know it for your good here, by submission, or to your cost hereafter.

The Decrees of God

All that is intended when we say that God decrees all that comes to pass is that all events are subject to the disposals of Providence, or that God orders all things in His providence, that He intended from eternity to order all things in Providence, and intended to order them as He does. (Whether God has decreed all things that ever came to pass or not, all who own the being of a god own that He knows all things beforehand. Now it is self-evident that if He knows all things beforehand, He either approves of them or He does not approve of them. He is either willing that they should be, or He is not willing that they should be. But to will that they should be is to decree them)

The Foreknowledge of God: It is most certain that if there are any things so contingent that there is an equal possibility of their being or not being, so that they may be or may not be, God foreknows from all eternity that they may be, and also that they may not be. All will grant that we need no revelation to teach us this. And furthermore, if God knows all things that are to come to pass, He also foreknows whether those contingent things are come to pass or not at the same time that they are contingent, and that they may or may not come to pass. But what a contradiction is it to say that God knows a thing will come to pass and yet, at the same time, knows that it is contingent whether it will come to pass or not. That is to say, He certainly knows it will come to pass, and yet certainly knows it may not come to pass! What a contradiction is it to say that God certainly foreknew that Judas would betray his Master or Peter deny Him, and yet certainly knew that it might be otherwise, or certainly knew that He might be deceived! I suppose it will be acknowledged by all that for God certainly to know a thing will be, and yet certainly to know that it may not be, is the same thing as certainly to know that He may be deceived. I suppose it will also be acknowledged that certainly to know a thing, and also at the same time to know that we may be deceived in it, is the same thing as certainly to know it, and certainly to know that we are uncertain of it, or that we do not certainly know it; and that it is the same thing as certainly to know it, and not certainly to know it at the same time, which we leave to be considered whether it is not a contradiction.

God foreknows the elect, as God is said to know those that are His own sheep from strangers, and as Christ is said not to know the workers of iniquity, that is, He does not own them as belonging to Him. In the same sense, God is said to know the elect from all eternity: that is, He knew them as a man knows his own things. He acknowledged them from eternity. He owns them as His children. Reprobates He did not know; they were strangers to God from all eternity.

(The foreknowledge of God will necessarily infer a decree; for God could not foreknow that things would be unless He had decreed they should be,) and that because things would not be future unless He had decreed they should be. If God, from all eternity, knew that such and such things were future, then they were future, and consequently the proposition was from all eternity true that such a thing, at such a time, would be. And it is as impossible that a thing should be future, without some reason of its being future, as that it should actually be, without some reason why it is. It is as perfectly unreasonable to suppose that this proposition should be true—that such a thing will be, or is to be, without a reason why it is true—as it is that this proposition should be true: such a thing actually is, or has been, without some reason why that is true, or why that thing exists. For as the being of the thing is not in its own nature necessary, so that proposition that was true before (that it shall be) is not in its own nature a necessary truth. Therefore I draw this consequence: that if there must be some reason of why a thing is future, it can be nothing other than God's decree; that such a thing will be has been determined by God.

Either things are future antecedently to God's decree and independent of it or they are not. If they are not future antecedently to and independent of God's decree, then they are made so by His decree; there is no middle ground. But if they are so antecedent to His decree, then this absurdity will follow, that God has no power by His decree to make anything future or not future. He has no choice in the case. And if it is already decided, something must have decided it, for something cannot be true without a reason why it is true. And if something has determined or decided the truth of it, it must be God who has decided it, or something else. It cannot be chance or mere accident; that is contrary to very rational supposition. For it is to be supposed that there is some reason for it, and that something decides it. If there is anything that come to pass by mere accident, then it comes to pass of itself without any reason. If it is not chance therefore that has decided it, it must be God or the creature. It cannot be the creature as actually existing, for, by supposition, it is determined from all eternity before any creature exists. Therefore, if it is anything in the creature that decides it in any way, it must be only the futurition of that thing in the creature. But this brings us to the absurdity and contradiction that the same thing is both the cause and the effect of itself. The very effect, the cause of which we are seeking, is the futurition of the thing,

and if this futurition is the cause of that effect, it is the
cause of itself.

If God does not know all things, then His knowledge may increase. He may gain knowledge, and may
grow wiser as He grows older. He may discover new
things, and may draw consequences from them. And
He may be mistaken; if He does not know, He may
guess wrong; and if He does not know, He has no infallible judgment, for an infallible judgment is from full
knowledge. If He may be mistaken, He may order matters wrong, He may be frustrated, and His measures may
be broken. For, doubtless, in things that are uncertain,
He orders things according to what appears most probable or else He fails in prudence. But in so ordering
things, His measures may be broken. And then the
greater part of the great events would be uncertain to
Him for the greater part of them depend on men's free
actions. That He does foreknow is evident by His predicting and foretelling events, and even the sins of
men, such as Judas's sin. If He did not foreknow, He
might change His will as He altered His views. Now it is
especially with respect to God's will and purposes that
He is said in Scripture not to be changeable.

That election is not from a foresight of works, or
conditional, as depending on the condition of man's
will, is evident by 2 Timothy 1:9: "Who hath saved us,
and called us with a holy calling, not according to our
works, but according to His own purpose and grace,
which was given us in Christ Jesus before the world be-
gan." Philippians 2:13: "For it is God that worketh in
you, both to will and to do of His own good pleasure."
Romans 9:15–16: "I will have mercy on whom I will have
mercy, and will have compassion on whom I will have
compassion. So then, it is not of him that willeth, nor
of him that runneth, but of God that showeth mercy."
Men's labors and endeavors themselves are from God.

1 Corinthians 15:10: "But by the grace of God, I am what I am; and His grace, which was bestowed upon me, was not in vain; but I labored more abundantly than they all. Yet not I, but the grace of God which was with me."

Contingency, as it is held by some, is at the same time contradicted by them if they hold to foreknowledge. This is all that follows from an absolute, unconditional, irreversible decree, that it is impossible but that the things decreed should be. The same exactly follows from foreknowledge, that it is absolutely impossible but that the thing certainly foreknown should precisely come to pass.

The Election of God: If God ever determined that some of mankind should certainly be saved, and did not leave it altogether undetermined whether ever so much as one soul of all mankind should believe in Christ, it must be that He determined that some particular persons should certainly believe in Him. For it is certain that if He has left it undetermined concerning this and that and the other person, whether ever he should believe or not, and so of every particular person in the world, then there is no necessity at all that this or that or any particular person in the world should ever be saved by Christ through any determination of God's. So that though God sent His Son into the world, yet the matter was left altogether undetermined by God whether ever any person should be saved by Him, and there was all this ado about Christ's birth, death, resurrection, ascension, and sitting at God's right hand, when it was not as yet determined whether He should ever save one soul, or have any mediatorial kingdom at all.

It is most absurd to call such an election based upon God's foreknowledge of who would believe by the name of "election," seeing there is a necessary connection between faith in Jesus Christ and eternal life. Those who believe in Christ must be saved, according to God's inviolable constitution of things. What nonsense is it, therefore, to talk of choosing such to life from all eternity out of the rest of mankind! A predestination of such to life is altogether useless and needless. By faith in one who has bought eternal life for them, they have, of unavoidable consequence, a right to eternal life. Now what sense is it to say that God has, from all eternity, of His free grace, chosen out those who He foresaw would have no guilt of sin, that they should not be punished for their guilt, as others were, when it is a contradiction to suppose that they can be punished for their guilt when they have none? For who can lay anything to their charge when it is Christ who has died? And what do they mean by an election of men to that which is, in its own nature, impossible that it should not be, whether they are elected to it or no, or by God's choosing them who had a right to eternal life, that they should possess it? What sense is it to say that a creditor chooses out those among his debtors to be free from debt who owe him nothing? But if they say that election is only God's determination that all who believe shall be saved, in what sense can this be called election? They are not persons who are here chosen, but mankind is divided into two sorts, believing and unbelieving, and God chooses the believing ones. It is not election of persons, but of qualifications. God does from all eternity choose to bestow eternal life upon those who have a right to it, rather than upon those who have a right to damnation. Is this all the election we have an account of in God's Word? Such a thing as election may well be allowed, for that there is such a thing as sovereign love is certain: that is, love not for any excelleny, but merely God's good pleasure. For whether it is proper to say that God from all eternity loved the elect or not, it is proper to say that God loved men after the fall while sinners and enemies. For God so loved the world that He gave His only begotten Son to die. This was not for any goodness or excellency, but merely God's good pleasure, for He would not love the fallen angels.

God's loving some and not others, antecedent to any manner of difference in them why He should love one more than the other, may appear reasonable thus: God of His own natural disposition really loves His reasonable creatures. Therefore his love to us before the foundation of the world is not merely an act of His wisdom, pleasing to make some happy and not others, as some have seemed to suppose, but real love such as ours, but only infinitely more sweet and pure, and void of all imperfection. Now God in His wisdom sees it best that all should not be His, which is the same thing as to God as an absolute impossibility. Now we find by experience, that however our natural disposition would lead us to love these or those, as to any qualification in them, yet if circumstances are such that we never in the least conceived that there could be any possibility of their being ours, we find no disposition to love them. Though divine things aren't like human things, yet comparison from one to the other may in some cases help us to conceive.

If there is no election, then it is not God that makes men to differ, expressly contrary to Scripture. No man ought to praise God for that happiness that he has above other men, or for that distinction that is between him and other men, that he is holy and that he is saved, when they are not holy and not saved. When the saints in heaven look on the devils in hell, they have no occasion to praise God on account of the difference between them. Some of the ill consequences of the Arminian doctrines are that they rob God of the greater

part of the glory of His grace, and take away any principal motive to love and praise Him; they exalt man to
God's level, and ascribe the glory to self that belongs to
God alone. Romans 11:7: "The election hath obtained,
and the rest were blinded." That by election here is not
meant the Gentiles, but the elect part of the Jews, is
most apparent by the context. Arminians who allow
that some only are elect, and not all are saved, but none
are reprobate, overthrow hereby their own main objections against reprobation, viz., that God allows salvation to all, and encourages them to seek it, which, say
they, would be inconsistent with God's truth if He had
absolutely determined not to save them. For they will
not deny that those who are elect while ungodly are
warned by God to beware of eternal damnation, and to
avoid such and such things lest they should be
damned. But for God to warn men to beware of damnation, though He has absolutely determined that they
shall not be damned, is exactly parallel with His exhort-
ing men to seek salvation, though He has actually determined that they shall not be saved.

The Arminian notion of election is that when the
apostles speak of election, they only mean that by
which the professing Christians in those days were distinguished from others, as the nation of Israel of old
was. This is unreasonable according to their own principles. For if they were elected, and that was the reason
why they so far embraced the gospel as to become
Christians rather than others, then, on Arminian principles, no thanks were due to them for embracing the
gospel; neither were others who continued openly to
reject the gospel to blame. And it was in vain to use any
means to persuade any to join with the Christian
Church, nor were any to blame for not doing it, or to be
praised for doing it. Besides, their principles render
vain all endeavors to spread the gospel. For the gospel

will certainly be spread to all nations that are elect, and
all such shall have the offers of the gospel whether they
take care of the matter or no.

It is evident that the apostle, in Romans 9, does not
have respect only to God's sovereignty in the election
and preterition of nations, because he illustrates his
meaning by the instance of a particular person,
Pharaoh. The exercise of the sovereignty that he speaks
of appears by the express words of the apostle about vessels of mercy and vessels of wrath, vessels of honor and
vessels of dishonor. But the vessels of mercy, he speaks
of as prepared to glory. They, it is plain, are those who
shall be saved, and the vessels of wrath are those who
perish. He speaks of those who shall be saved in
Romans 9:27: "A remnant shall be saved." What is there
that God decrees, according to the scheme of the
Arminians, so as to make it in any measure consistent
with itself? He does not decree any of the great events
of the world of mankind (which are the principal
events, and those to which all others are subordinated),
because these depend on men's free will. He does not
absolutely decree any events wherein the welfare of
men is concerned, for if He does then these things, according to their scheme, cannot be the subject of
prayer. For according to them, it is absurd to seek or
pray for things which we do not know but that God has
absolutely decreed and fixed before. We do not know
but that He has determined absolutely and unfrustrata-
bly from eternity that they shall not be, and then, by
their scheme, we cannot pray in faith for them. And if
God does not decree and order those events
beforehand, then what becomes of the providence of
God, and what room is there for prayer, if there is no
providence? Prayer is shut out this way also. According
to them, we cannot reasonably pray for the accom-
plishment of things that are already fixed before our

prayers. For then our prayers alter nothing, and what, say they, signifies it for us to pray?

If God absolutely determined that Christ's death should have success in gathering a church for Him, it will follow that there was a number absolutely elected, or that God had determined some should surely be saved. If God determined that some should surely be saved, that implies that He had determined that He would see to it that some would perform the conditions of salvation and be saved, or, which is the same thing, that He would cause that they should be surely saved. But this cannot be without fixing on the persons beforehand, for the cause is before the effect. There is no such thing as God's resolving absolutely beforehand that He would save some, and yet not determining who they should be before they were actually saved; or that He should see to it that there should be in a number the requisites of salvation, and yet not determine who till they actually have the requisites of salvation. But God had absolutely determined that some should be saved, yea, a great number, after Christ's death, and had determined it beforehand because He had absolutely promised it (Isaiah 49:6 and 53:10; Titus 2:14). God, then, having absolutely purposed this before Christ's death, must either have determined the persons, or resolved that He would hereafter determine the persons—at least, if He saw there was need of it, and saw that they did not come in of themselves. But this latter supposition, if we allow it, overthrows the Arminian scheme. It shows that such a predetermination, or absolute election, is not inconsistent with God's perfections, the nature of the gospel-constitution, or God's government of the world, His promise of reward to the believing and obedient, and the design of gospel offers and commands, as the Arminians suppose. If God has absolutely determined to save some certain persons, then, doubtless, He has in like manner determined concerning all who are to be saved. God's promising supposes not only that the thing is future, but that God will do it. If it is left to chance or man's contingent will, and the event happens right, God is never the truer. He does not perform His promise. He takes no effectual care about it; it is not He who promised that performed it. That thing, or rather nothing, called "fortune" orders all.

The Decrees of God and the Will of God: Arminians ridicule the distinction between the secret and revealed will of God, or, more properly expressed, the distinction between the decree and law of God, because we say He may decree one thing and command another. And so, they argue, we hold a contrariety in God, as if one will of His contradicted another. However, if they will call this a contradiction of wills, we know that there is such a thing, so that it is the greatest absurdity to dispute about it. We and they know it was God's secret will that Abraham should not sacrifice his son Isaac, yet His command was that he should do it. We know that God willed that Pharaoh's heart should be hardened, and yet that the hardness of his heart was sin. We know that God willed the Egyptians should hate God's people. Psalm 105:25: "He turned their heart to hate His people, and deal subtly with His servants." We know that it was God's will that Absalom should lie with David's wives. 2 Samuel 12:11: "Thus saith the Lord, 'I will raise up this evil against thee, out of thine own house; and I will take thy wives before thine eyes, and give them unto thy neighbor; and he shall lie with thy wives in the sight of this sun. For thou didst it secretly; but I will do this thing before all Israel, and before the sun.' " We know that God willed that Jeroboam and the ten tribes should rebel. The same may be said of the plunder of the Babylonians, and other instances might be given. The Scripture plainly tells us that God wills to harden some men (Romans 9:18). He willed that Christ should be killed by men.

When a distinction is made between God's revealed will and His secret will, or His will of command and decree, "will" is certainly in that distinction taken in two senses. His will of decree is not His will in the same sense as His will of command is. Therefore, it is no difficulty at all to suppose that the one may be otherwise than the other. His will in both senses is His inclination, but when we say that He wills virtue, or loves virtue, or the happiness of His creature, thereby is intended that virtue, or the creature's happiness, absolutely and simply considered, is agreeable to the inclination of His nature. His will of decree is His inclination to a thing, not as to that thing absolutely and simply, but with respect to the universality of things that have been, are, or shall be. So God, though He hates a thing as it is simply, may incline to it with reference to the universality of things. Though He hates sin in itself, yet He may will to permit it for the greater promotion of holiness in this universality, including all things and at all times. So though He has no inclination to a creature's misery, considered absolutely, yet He may will it for the greater promotion of happiness in this universality. God inclines to excellency, which is harmony, yet He may incline to suffer that which is unharmonious in itself for the promotion of universal harmony, or for the promoting of the harmony that there is in the universality, and making it shine the brighter. And thus it must be, and no hypothesis whatsoever will relieve a man, but that he must own these two wills of God. For all must own that God sometimes wills not to hinder the breach of His own commands because He does not in fact hinder it. He wills to permit sin, it is evident, because He does permit it. None will say that God Himself does what He does not will to do.

But, you will say, "God wills to permit sin, since He wills the creature should be left to his freedom. And if He should hinder it, He would offer violence to the nature of His own creature."

I answer, this comes nevertheless to the very thing that I say. You say that God does not will sin absolutely, but rather than alter the law of nature and the nature of free agents He wills it. (He wills what is contrary to excellency in some particulars for the sake of a more general excellency and order.) So that this scheme of the Arminians does not help the matter at all.

The Decrees of God and Evil: It cannot be any injustice in God to determine who is certainly to sin, and so who is certainly to be damned. For if we suppose this impossibility, that God had not determined anything, things would happen as fatally as they do now. For as to such an absolute contingency, which they attribute to man's will, calling it the sovereignty of the will; if they mean by this sovereignty of will that a man can will as he wills, it is perfect nonsense, and is the same as if they should spend an abundance of time and pains, and be very hot, at proving that a man can will when he wills, that is, that it is possible for that to be which is. But if they mean that there is a perfect contingency in the will of man, that is, that it happens merely by chance that a man wills such a thing and not another, it is an impossibility and contradiction that a thing should be without any cause or reason, and when there was in every way as much cause why it should not have been. Wherefore, seeing things unavoidably go fatally and necessarily, what injustice is it in the Supreme Being, seeing it is a contradiction that it should be otherwise, to decree that they should be as they are!

That we should say that God has decreed every action of men, yea, every action that is sinful, and every circumstance of those actions; that He predetermines that they shall be in every respect as they afterwards are; that He determines that there shall be such actions, and just so sinful as they are, and yet that God does not decree the actions that are sinful, as sin, but decrees them as good—all of this is really consistent. For we do not mean by decreeing an action as sinful, I mean decreeing it for the sake of the sinfulness of the action. God decrees that they shall be sinful for the sake of the good that He causes to arise from the sinfulness thereof, whereas man decrees them for the sake of the evil that is in them.

Nor do we say that God may do evil that good may come of it. I do not argue that God may commit evil that good may come of it, but that He may will that evil should come to pass, and permit that it may come to pass, that good may come of it. It is in itself absolutely evil for any being to commit evil that good may come of it. But it would be no evil, but good, even in a creature, to will that evil should come to pass if he had sufficient wisdom to see certainly that good would come of it, or that more good would come to pass in that way than in any other. And the only reason why it would not be lawful for a creature to permit evil to come to pass, and that it would not be wise, good, and virtuous in him so to do, is that he does not have perfect wisdom and sufficiency so as to render it fitting that such an affair should be trusted with him. In so doing he goes beyond his line; he goes out of his province; he meddles with things too high for him. It is everyone's duty to do things fitting for him in his sphere, and commensurate to his power. God never entrusted this providence in the hands of creatures of finite understandings, nor is it proper that He should.

If a prince were of perfect and all-comprehensive wisdom and foresight, and he should see that an act of treason would be for the great advancement of the welfare of his kingdom, it might be wise and virtuous in him to will that such act of treason should come to pass. Yea, it would be foolish and wrong if he did not; and it would be prudent and wise in him not to restrain the traitor, but to let him alone to go in the way he chose. And yet he might hate the treason at the same time, and he might properly also give forth laws at the same time forbidding it upon pain of death, and might hold these laws in force against this traitor.

The Arminians themselves allow that God permits sin, and that, if He permits it, it will come to pass. So the only difficulty about the act of the will that is in it is that God should will evil to be so that good may come of it. But it is demonstrably true that if God sees that good will come of it, and more good than otherwise, so that when the whole series of events is viewed by God and all things balanced, the sum total of good with the evil is more than without it, all being subtracted that needs be subtracted, and added that is to be added; and if the sum total of good thus considered is greatest, greater than the sum in any other case, then it will follow that God, if He is a wise and holy being, must will it.

For if this sum total that has evil in it, when what the evil subtracts is subtracted has yet the greatest good in it, then it is the best sum total, better than the other sum total that has no evil in it. But if, all things considered, it is really the best, how can it be otherwise than that it should be chosen by an infinitely wise and good Being, whose holiness and goodness consists in always choosing what is best? Which does it argue most, wisdom or folly, a good disposition or an evil one, when two things are set before a being, the one better and the other worse, to choose the worse and refuse the better?

There is no inconsistency or contrariety between the decretive and perceptive will of God. It is very consistent to suppose that God may hate the thing itself, and yet will that it should come to pass. Yea, I do not fear to assert that the thing itself may be contrary to God's will, and yet that it may be agreeable to His will that it should come to pass, because His will, in the one case, has not the same object with His will in the other case. To suppose God to have contrary wills towards the same object is a contradiction, but it is not so to suppose Him to have contrary wills about different objects. The thing itself, and that the thing should come to pass, are different, as is evident, because it is possible that the one may be good and the other may be evil. The thing itself may be evil, and yet it may be a good thing that it should come to pass. It may be a good thing that an evil thing should come to pass, and oftentimes it most certainly and undeniably is so, and proves to be so.

Objectors to the doctrine of election may say that God cannot always preserve men from sinning unless He destroys their liberty. But will they deny that an omnipotent, infinitely wise God could possibly invent and set before men such strong motives to obedience, and keep them before them in such a manner as should influence them to continue in their obedience, as the elect angels have done, without destroying their liberty? God will order it so that the saints and angels in heaven never will sin, and does it therefore follow that their liberty is destroyed, and that they are not free, but forced in their actions? Does it follow that they are turned into machines and blocks, as the Arminians say the Calvinistic doctrines turn men into?

I wish the reader to consider the unreasonableness of rejecting plain revelations just because they are puzzling to our reason. There is no greater difficulty attending this doctrine than the contrary, nor so great. So that, though the doctrine of the decrees is mysterious, and attended with difficulties, yet the opposite doctrine is in itself more mysterious, and attended with greater difficulties, and with contradictions to reason more evident to one who thoroughly considers things so that even if the Scripture had made no revelation of it, we would have had reason to believe it. But since the Scripture is so abundant in declaring it, the unreasonableness of rejecting it appears the more glaring.

The sin of crucifying Christ being foreordained of God in His decree, and ordered in His providence, of which we have abundant evident from the nature of the thing, and from the great ends God had to accomplish by means of this wicked act of crucifying Christ; it being, as it were, the cause of all the decrees, the greatest of all decreed events, and that on which all other decreed events depend as their main foundation; being the main thing in that greatest work of God, the work of redemption, which is the end of all other works; and it being so much prophesied of, and so plainly spoken of, as being done according to the determinate counsel and foreknowledge of God—I say, seeing we have such evidence that this sin is foreordained in God's decrees, and ordered in providence, and it being, as it were, the head sin and representative of the sin of men in general, hence is a clear argument that all the sins of men are foreordained and ordered by a wise Providence. Hence God decrees from all eternity, to permit all the evil that ever he does permit, because God's permitting is God's forbearing to act or to prevent.

The commands and prohibitions of God are only significations of our duty and of His nature. It is ac-

knowledged that sin is, in itself considered, infinitely
contrary to God's nature, but it does not follow but that
it may be the pleasure of God to permit it for the sake of
the good that He will bring out of it. God can bring
such good out of that, which in itself is contrary to His
nature, and which, in itself considered, He abhors, as
may be very agreeable to His nature; and when sin is
spoken of as contrary to the will of God, it is contrary to
His will, considered only as in itself. As man commits
it, it is contrary to God's will, for men act in committing it with a view to that which is evil. But as God permits it, it is not contrary to God's will, for God in permitting it has respect to the great good that He will
make it an occasion of. If God respected sin as man respects it in committing it, it would be exceedingly contrary to His will, but considered as God decrees to permit it, it is not contrary to God's will. For example, the
crucifying of Christ was a great sin, and, as man committed it, it was exceedingly hateful and highly provoking to God. Yet upon many great considerations, it was
the will of God that it should be done. Will anybody say
that it was not the will of God that Christ should be
crucified? Acts 4:28: "For to do whatsoever Thy hand
and Thy counsel determined before to be done."

Sin is an evil, yet the futurition of sin, or that sin
should be future, is not an evil thing. Evil is an evil
thing, and yet it may be a good thing that evil should
be in the world. There is certainly a difference between
the thing itself existing, and its being an evil thing that
ever it came into existence. For instance, it might be an
evil thing to crucify Christ, yet it was a good thing that
the crucifying of Christ came to pass. As men's act, it
was evil, but as God ordered it, it was good. Who will
deny but that it may be true that evil's coming to pass
may be an occasion of greater good than it is an evil,
and so of there being more good in the whole than if

that evil had not come to pass? And if so, then it is a good thing that that evil comes to pass. When we say the thing is an evil thing in itself, then we mean that it is evil, considering it only within its own bounds. But when we say that it is a good thing that ever it came to pass, then we consider the thing as a thing among events, or as one thing belonging to the series of events, and as related to the rest of the series. If a man should say that it was a good thing that ever it happened that Joseph's brethren sold him into Egypt, or that it was a good thing that ever it came to pass that Pope Leo X sent out indulgences for the commission of future sins, nobody would understand a man thus expressing himself as justifying these acts.

It implies no contradiction to suppose that an act may be an evil act, and yet that it is a good thing that such an act should come to pass. A man may have been a bad man, and yet it may be a good thing that there has been such a man. This implies no contradiction, because it implies no contradiction to suppose that there being such a man may be an occasion of there being more good in the whole than there would have been otherwise. So it no more implies a contradiction to suppose that an action may be a bad action, and yet that it may be a good thing that there has been such an action. God's commands, calls, and counsels imply that it is our duty to do these things, and though they may be our duty, yet it may be certain beforehand that we shall not do them.

And if there is any difficulty in this, the same difficulty will attend the scheme of the Arminians, for they allow that God permits sin. Therefore, as He permits it, it cannot be contrary to His will. For if it were contrary to His will as He permits it, then it would be contrary to His will to permit it, for that is the same thing. But nobody will say that God permits sin when it is against His will to permit it, for this would be to make Him act involuntarily, or against His own will.

If God restrains sin when He pleases and, when He permits it, permits it for the sake of some good that it will be an occasion of, and actually restrains in all other cases, it is evident that when He permits it, it is His will that it should come to pass for the sake of the good that it will be an occasion of. If He permits it for the sake of that good, then He does not permit it merely because He would infringe on the creature's liberty in restraining it. It is further evident because He does restrain it when that good is not in view. If it is His will to permit it to come to pass for the sake of the good that its coming to pass will be an occasion of, then it is His will to permit it so that, by its coming to pass, He may obtain that good. And therefore it must necessarily be His will that it should come to pass so that He may obtain that good. If He permits it, so that by its coming to pass He may obtain a certain good, then His proximate end in permitting it is that it may come to pass. And if He wills the means for the sake of the end, He therein wills the end. If God wills to permit a thing so that it may come to pass, then He wills that it should come to pass. This is self-evident. But if He wills to permit it to come to pass so that, by its coming to pass, He may obtain some end, then He wills to permit it that it should come to pass. For to will to permit a thing to come to pass so that, by its coming to pass, good may be obtained is exactly the same thing as to will to permit it to come to pass so that it may come to pass, and so the end may be attained. To will to permit a thing to come to pass so that He may obtain some end by its coming to pass, and yet to be unwilling that it should come to pass, certainly implies a contradiction.

The Arminian's other objection is that God's decrees make God the author of sin. I answer that there is no more necessity of supposing God to be the author of sin on this scheme than on the other. For if we suppose that God has determined from all eternity the number and persons of those who shall perform the condition of the covenant of grace, then in order to support this doctrine there is no need of maintaining any more concerning God's decreeing sin than that God has decreed that He will permit all the sin that ever comes to pass, and that, upon His permitting it, it will certainly come to pass.

And they hold the same thing, for they hold that God determines beforehand to permit all the sin that comes to pass, and that He certainly knows that if He permits it, it will come to pass. In their scheme they allow both of these: They allow that God permits all the sin to come to pass that ever does come to pass, and those who allow the foreknowledge of God also allow the other thing, that He knows, concerning all the sin that ever does really come to pass, that it will come to pass upon His permitting it. So if this is making God the author of sin, they make Him so in the very same way that they charge us with doing it.

Another objection against God's decreeing or ordering in any sense that sin should come to pass is that man cannot do this without making God Himself sinful, and in some measure guilty of the sin, and that therefore God cannot. To this I answer that the same objection lies against their own scheme in two ways: First, they own that God permits sin, that He determines to permit it beforehand, and that He knows, with respect to all sin that ever is committed, that upon His permitting it, it will come to pass—and we hold no other. Second, their objection is that what is a sin in men is a sin in God, and therefore in any sense to decree sin would be a sin. But if this objection is good, it is as strong against God's permission of sin, which they allow, for it would be a sin in men to permit sin. We ought not to permit or suffer it where we have an opportunity to hinder it, and we cannot permit it without making ourselves in some measure guilty. Yet they allow that God permits sin, and that His permitting it does not make Him guilty of it. Why must the argument from men to God be stronger in the other case than in this?

God decrees all things, and even all sins. Even the free actions of men are subject to God's disposal. What men determine never comes to pass unless God determines it. God determines the limits of men's lives. This is exceedingly evident from Job 7:1: "Is there not an appointed time to man upon earth? Are not his days also like the days of a hireling?" Days of a hireling signify an appointed, certain, limited time, as in Isaiah 16:14 and 21:16. If the limits of men's lives are determined, men's free actions must be determined, and even their sins, for their lives often depend on such acts (see also Job 14:5).

The Decrees of God and Means: It is commonly said that God decrees nothing upon a foresight of anything in the creature, since this, they say, argues imperfection in God; and so it does, taken in the sense that they commonly intend it. But nobody, I believe, will deny but that God decrees many things that He would not have decreed if He had not foreknown and foredetermined such and such other things. What we mean, we completely express thus: God decrees all things harmoniously and in excellent order; one thing harmonizes with another, and there is such a relation between all the decrees as makes the most excellent order. So we say something like, "God decrees rain in drought because He decrees the earnest prayers of His people, or He decrees the prayers of His people because

He decrees rain." I acknowledge that to say that "God decrees a thing because. . ." is an improper way of speaking, but no more improper than all our other ways of speaking about God. God decrees the latter event because of the former no more than He decrees the former because of the latter. What we mean is this: When God decrees to give the blessing of rain, He decrees the prayers of His people; and when He decrees the prayers of His people for rain, He very commonly decrees rain. And thereby there is harmony between these two decrees, of rain and the prayers of God's people. Thus also, when He decrees diligence and industry, He decrees riches and prosperity; when He decrees prudence, He often decrees success; when He decrees striving, then He often decrees the obtaining of the kingdom of heaven; when He decrees the preaching of the gospel, then He decrees the bringing home of souls to Christ; when He decrees good natural faculties, diligence, and good advantages, then He decrees learning; when He decrees summer, then He decrees the growing of plants; when He decrees conformity to His Son, then He decrees calling; when He decrees calling, then He decrees justification; and when He decrees justfication, then He decrees everlasting glory. Thus, all the decrees of God are harmonious, and this is all that can be said for or against absolute or conditional decrees. But this I say, it is as improper to make one decree a condition of another as to make the other a condition of that; but there is harmony between both.

Those opposed to this say, "To what purpose are praying, striving, and attending on means, if all was irreversibly determined by God beforehand?" But to say that all was determined before these prayers and strivings is a very wrong way of speaking, and begets those ideas in the mind which correspond with no realities with respect to God. The decrees of our everlasting state were not before our prayers and strivings, for these are as much present with God from all eternity as they are the moment they are present with us. They are present as part of His decrees, or rather as the same, and they did as really exist in eternity with respect to God, as they exist in time, and as much at one time as another. Therefore, we can no more fairly argue that these will be in vain because God has foredetermined all things than we can that they would be in vain if they existed as soon as the decree, for so they do, inasmuch as they are a part of it.

God decrees all the good that ever comes to pass, and therefore there certainly will come to pass no more good than he has absolutely decreed to cause. And there certainly and infallibly will no more believe, nor more be godly, and no more be saved than God has decreed that He will cause to believe and cause to be godly, and will save.

The first objection of the Arminians is that the divine decrees infringe on the creature's liberty. In answer to this objection, we may observe some things to show what is the true notion of liberty, and the absurdity of their notion of liberty. Their notion of liberty is that there is a sovereignty in the will, and that the will determines itself, so that its determination to choose or refuse this or that is primarily within itself, which description of liberty implies a self-contradiction. For it supposes the will in its first act choosing or refusing to be determined by itself, which implies that there is an antecedent act of the will to that first act, determining that act. For if the will determines its own first act, then there must be an act of the will before that first act (for that determining is acting), which is a contradiction. There can be no fallacy in this, for we know that if the will determines its own act, it does not determine it without acting. Therefore, here is the contradiction:

there is an act of the will before the first act. There is
an act of the will determining what it shall choose before the first act of choice, which is as much as to say
that there is an act of volition before the first act of volition. For the will's determining what it will choose is
choosing. The will's determining what it will will is
willing. So that, according to this notion of liberty, the
will must choose before it chooses in order to determine what it will choose. If the will determines itself, it
is certain that one act must determine another. If the
will determines its own choice, then it must determine
by a foregoing act what it will choose. If the will determines its own act, then an antecedent act determines
the consequent, for that determining is acting. The
will cannot determine without acting.

Therefore I inquire what determines that first act of
the will, that is, its determination of its own act? It must
be answered, according to their scheme, that it is the
will by a foregoing act. Here again we have the same
contradiction, that the first act of the will is determined by an act that is before that first act. If the will
determines itself, or determines its own choice, the
meaning of it must be (if there is any meaning belonging to it) that the will determines how it will choose,
and that it chooses according to that its own determination how to choose, or is directed in choosing by
that its own determination.

But then I would inquire whether that first determination that directs the choice is not itself an act or a
volition; and, if so, I would inquire what determines
that act? Is it another determination still prior to that
in the order of nature? Then I would inquire, what determines the first act or determination of all? If the will
in its acts of willing or choosing determines or directs
itself how to choose, then there is something done by
the will prior to its act of choosing that is determined,

its determining or directing itself how to choose. This act of determining or directing must be something besides or distinct from the choice determined or directed, and must be prior in order of nature to it.

Here are two acts of the will, one the cause of the other, that is, the act of the will directing and determining, and the act or choice directed or determined. Now, I inquire, what determines that first act of the will determining or directing to determine and direct as it does? If it is said that the will determines itself in that, then that supposes there is another act of the will prior to that, directing and determining that act which is contrary to the supposition. And if it was not, still the question would recur, what determines that first determining act of the will?

If the will determines itself, one of these three things must be meant:

1. The very same act of the will determines itself. But this is as absurd as to say that something makes itself, and it supposes it to be before it is. For the act of determining is as much prior to the thing determined as the act of making is before the thing made.

2. Or the meaning must be that the will determines its own act by some other act that is prior to it in order of nature, which implies that the will acts before its first act.

3. Or the meaning must be that the faculty, considered at the same time as perfectly without act, determines its own consequent act, which is to talk without a meaning, and is a great absurdity. To suppose that the faculty, remaining at the same time perfectly without act, can determine anything is a plain contradiction, for determining is acting. And besides, if the will does determine itself, that power of determining itself does not argue any freedom, unless it is by an act of the will, or unless that determination is itself an act of choice.

For what freedom or liberty is there in the will's determining itself without an act of choice in determining,
whereby it may choose which way it will determine itself? So that those who suppose the will has a power of
self-determination must suppose that that very determination is an act of the will, or an act of choice, or
else it does not at all help them out in what they would
advocate, which is the liberty of the will. But if that very
determination how to act is itself an act of choice, the
question returns, what determines this act of choice?

Also, the foreknowledge of God contradicts their
notion of liberty as much, and in every respect in the
same manner, as a decree. For they do not pretend that
decree contradicts liberty any otherwise than as it infers that it is beforehand certain that the thing will
come to pass, and that it is impossible but that it
should be, as the decree makes an indissoluble connection beforehand between the subject and predicate of
the proposition that such a thing shall be. A decree infers no other necessity than that. And God's foreknowledge infers the same, for all intents and purposes. For if from all eternity God foreknew that such a
thing would be, then the event was infallibly certain beforehand, and that proposition was true from all eternity that such a thing would be. And therefore there
was an indissoluble connection beforehand between
the subject and predicate of that proposition. If the
proposition was true beforehand, the subject and predicate of it were connected beforehand. And therefore it
follows that it is utterly impossible that it should not
prove true, and that, for this reason, that it is utterly
impossible that a thing should be true and not true at
the same time. *Law of Non-Contradiction*

The same kind of infallible certainty that the thing
will come to pass, or impossibility but that it should
come to pass, that they object against must necessarily

be inferred another way, whether we hold the thing to be in any way decreed or not. For it has been shown before, and I suppose none will deny, that God from all eternity decrees His own actions. Therefore He, from all eternity, decrees every punishment that He ever has inflicted or will inflict. So that it is impossible, by their own reasoning, but that the punishment should come to pass. And if it is impossible but that the punishment should come to pass, then it is equally impossible but that the sin should come to pass. For if it is possible that the sin should not come to pass, and yet impossible but that the punishment should come to pass, then it is impossible but that God should punish that sin which may never be.

For God certainly to know that a thing will be, that possibly may be and possibly may not be, implies a contradiction. If possibly it may be otherwise, then how can God know certainly that it will be? If it possibly may be otherwise, then He knows it possibly may be otherwise, and that it is inconsistent with His certainly knowing that it will not be otherwise. If God certainly knows it will be, and yet it may possibly be otherwise, then it may possibly happen to be otherwise than God certainly knows it will be. If so, then it may possibly happen that God may be mistaken in His judgment, when He certainly knows. For it is supposed that it is possible that it should be otherwise than He judges. For that it should be otherwise than He judges, and that He should be mistaken, are the same thing. How unfair therefore is it in those who hold the foreknowledge of God to insist upon this objection from human liberty against the decrees, when their scheme is attended with the same difficulty, exactly in the same manner!

They say, "As God's power extends only to all things possible, so God's knowledge only extends to all things knowable."

I answer, things impossible, or contradictions, are
not things; but events that come to pass are things.
God's power extends to all things, otherwise it would
not be infinite. So neither is the knowledge of God infinite unless God knows all things. To suppose that
God cannot do things that are impossible does not
suppose that God's power can be increased. But(to suppose that God does not know men's free actions supposes that God's knowledge may be increased.)To suppose that God's decrees are conditional, in the sense of
the Arminians, or that they depend, as they suppose, on
a foresight of something that shall come to pass in
time, is to suppose that something that first begins to
be in time is the cause of something that has been
from all eternity, which is absurd.)For nothing can be a
cause of that existence which is before the existence of
that cause. What an absurdity is it to suppose that that
existence which is an effect is effected by a cause, when
that cause that effects it is not, or has no being! If it is
answered that it is not the actual existence of the thing
that is the reason or cause of the decree, but the foresight of the existence; and the foresight of the existence may be at the same time with the decree, and before it, in the order of nature, though the existence itself is not; and that it is not properly the actual existence of the thing foreseen, that is the cause of the decree, but the existence of it in the divine foreknowledge—I reply that this does not help the difficulty at all,
but only puts it a step further off. For still, by their
scheme, the foreknowledge depends on the future actual existence, so that the actual existence is the cause
of the divine foreknowledge, which is infinite ages before it. And it is a great absurdity to suppose this effect
to flow from this cause before the existence of the
cause. And whatever is said, the absurdity will occur unless we suppose that the divine decree is the ground of

the futurition of the event, and also the ground of the foreknowlege of it. Then the cause is before the effect; but otherwise the effect is before the cause.

It is pretended that the antecedent certainty of any sin's being committed, seeing that it is attended with necessity, takes away all liberty, and makes warning and exhortations to avoid sin a mere illusion. To this I would bring the instance of Peter. Christ told him that he would surely deny Him thrice that night before the cock should crow twice. And yet, after that, Christ exhorted all His disciples to watch and pray so that they might not fall into temptation.

It is impossible for an infinitely wise and good Being to do otherwise than to choose what He sees on the whole to be best. And certainly reason requires us to suppose that of all possible events—with respect to sin, and the conversion and salvation of particular persons—it is better than one of those possible and opposite events should come to pass than another. And therefore, an infinitely wise and good Being must choose accordingly. What God permits, He decrees to permit. If it is no blemish to God to permit sin, then it is no blemish on Him to purpose or intend to permit it. And if He is omniscient, and designedly permits that sin which actually comes to pass, then he designedly permits that sin, knowing if He permits it, it will actually come to pass. And this is an effectual permission, and all that we plead for. What, then, do our adversaries quarrel with us for? And why do they pretend that we charge God with being the author of sin? There is a way of drawing consequences from Scripture that begs the question. As the Arminians say, there are many more texts plainly against election than seem to be for it, that is, those texts that represent that general offers of salvation are made as though it were left to men's choice whether they will be saved or not. But that is begging the question. For the question very much consists in these things: whether an absolute decree is inconsistent with man's liberty, and so with a general offer of salvation.

The Glory of God

God's glory, as it is spoken of in Scripture as the end of all God's works, is in the emanation of that fullness of God that is from eternity in God, *ad extra*, and towards those creatures that are capable of being sensible and active objects of such an emanation. It consists in communicating Himself to those two faculties of the understanding and will, by which faculties it is that creatures are sensible and active objects or subjects of divine emanations and communications.

God communicates Himself to the understanding in the manifestation that is made of the divine excellency, and the understanding, idea, or view which intelligent creatures have of it. He communicates His glory and fullness to the wills of sensible, willing, active beings in their rejoicing in the manifested glory of God; in their admiring it; in their loving God for it, and being in all respects affected and disposed suitably to such glory; their exercising and expressing those affections and dispositions wherein consists their praising and glorifying God; in their being themselves holy and having the image of this glory in their hearts, and as it were reflecting it as a jewel does the light of the sun, partaking of God's brightness; and in their being happy in God, whereby they partake of God's fullness of happiness.

This twofold emanation or communication of the divine fullness *ad extra* is answerable to the twofold emanation or going forth of the Godhead *ad intra*, wherein the internal and essential glory and fullness of the Godhead consists: the proceeding of the eternal Son of God, God's eternal idea and infinite understanding and wisdom, and the brightness of His glory, whereby

85

His beauty and excellency appear to Him, and the proceeding of the Holy Spirit or the eternal will, temper, disposition of the Deity, the infinite fullness of God's holiness, joy, and delight.

God is glorified within Himself in these two ways: (1) by appearing or being manifested to Himself in His own perfect idea, or in His Son, who is the brightness of His glory; and (2) by enjoying and delighting in Himself, by flowing forth in infinite love and delight towards Himself, or in His Holy Spirit.

So God glorifies Himself towards the creatures also in two ways: (1) by appearing to them, being manifested to their understanding; and (2) in communicating Himself to their hearts, and in their rejoicing and delighting in, and enjoying the manifestations which He makes of Himself. Both of them may be called His glory in the more extensive sense of the word: His shining forth, or the going forth of His excellency, beauty, and essential glory *ad extra.* By one way it goes forth towards their understandings, by the other it goes forth towards their wills or hearts.

God is glorified not only by His glory's being seen, but by its being rejoiced in. When those who see it delight in it, God is more glorified than if they only see it. His glory is then received by the whole soul, by both the understanding and by the heart. God made the world so that He might communicate (and the creature receive) His glory, and that it might be received by both the mind and heart. He who testifies his idea of God's glory does not glorify God so much as he who testifies also his approbation of and delight in it. Both these ways of God's glorifying Himself come from the same cause, the overflowing of God's internal glory, or an inclination in God to cause His internal glory to flow out *ad extra.* What God has in view in either of them, either in His manifesting His glory to the understanding, or His communication of it to the heart, is not that He may receive, but that He go forth. The main end of His shining forth is not that He may have His rays reflected back to Himself, but that the rays may go forth. And this is very consistent with what we are taught of God's being the Alpha and Omega, the first and the last. God made all things, and the end for which all things are made, and for which they are disposed, and for which they work continually, is that God's glory may shine forth and be received. From Him all creatures come, and in Him their well being consists. God is all their beginning, and God received is all their end. From Him and to Him are all things. They are all from Him, and they are all to be brought to Him. But it is not that they may add to Him, but that God might be received by them. The damned, indeed, are not immediately for God, but they are so ultimately. They are for the glorified saints and angels, and they for God, that God's glory may be manifested in them unto the vessels of mercy.

It is said that God has made all things for Himself, and in Revelation it is said they are created for God's pleasure. That is, they are made so that God may in them have occasion to fulfill His good pleasure in manifesting and communicating Himself. In this God takes delight, and for the sake of this delight God creates the world; but this delight is not properly from the creature's communication to God, but in God's to the creature. It is a delight in His own act. Let us explain the matter how we will, there is no way that the world can be for God more than so. For it cannot be that He can receive anything from the creature.

The great and universal end of God's creating the world was to communicate Himself. God is a communicating being. This communication is really only to intelligent beings. The communication of Himself to their understandings is His glory, and the communication of Himself with respect to their wills (the enjoying faculty) is their happiness. God created this world for the shining forth of His excellency, and for the flowing forth of His happiness. It does not make God the happier to be praised, but it is a becoming and condecent, worthy thing for infinite and supreme excellency to shine forth. It is not His happiness, but His excellency so to do. It is evident from the motive of God's creating the world, which could be nothing else but his goodness, that the end of man's creation must be happiness. If it is said that the end of man's creation might be that He might manifest His power, wisdom, holiness, or justice, I agree. But the question is, why God would make known His power, wisdom, and so on? What could move Him to will that there should be some beings that might know His power and wisdom? It could be nothing else but His goodness.

This is the question: What moved God to exercise and make known those attributes? We are not speaking of subordinate ends, but of the ultimate end or motive into which all others may be resolved. It is a very proper question to ask what attribute moved God to exert His power, but it is not proper to ask what moved God to exert His goodness, for this is the notion of goodness: an inclination to show goodness. Therefore, such a question would be no more proper than this: what inclined God to exert His inclination to exercise goodness? What nonsense, for it is asking and answering a question in the same words. God's power is shown no otherwise than by His powerfully bringing about some end. The very notion of wisdom is nicely contriving for an end; and if there is no end proposed, whatever is done is not wisdom. Therefore, if God created the world primarily from goodness, every whit of this goodness must necessarily ultimately terminate in the consciousness of the creature, for the world is in no other way capable of receiving goodness in any measure. But intelligent beings are the consciousness of the world. The end, therefore, of the creation must necessarily be that they may receive the goodness of God, and that they may be happy.

It appears also from the nature of happiness, which is the perception of excellency. For intelligent beings are created to be the consciousness of the universe, so that they may perceive what God is and does. This can be nothing else but to perceive the excellency of what He is and does. Yet He is nothing but excellency, and all that He does is nothing but excellent.

How then can it be said that God has made all things for Himself if it is certain that the highest end of the creation was the communication of happiness? I answer, that which is done for the gratifying of a natural inclination of God may very properly be said to be done for God. God takes complacence in communicating felicity, and He made all things for this complacence. His complacence in this making happy was the end of the creation. Revelation 4:11: "For Thy pleasure they are and were created." *Self Satisfaction*

We have proved that the end of the creation must be happiness, and the communication of the goodness of God, and that nothing but the Almighty's inclination to communicate His own happiness could be the motive for Him to create the world; and man or intelligent being is the immediate object of this goodness, and the subject of this communicated happiness. We have shown also that the Father's begetting of the Son is a complete communication of all His happiness, and so an eternal adequate and infinite exercise of perfect goodness that is completely equal to such an inclination in perfection.

Why then did God incline further to communicate

Himself, seeing He had done it infinitely and completely? Can there be an inclination to communicate goodness more than adequately to the inclination? To say so is to say that to communicate goodness adequately to the inclination is not yet adequate, inasmuch as He inclines to communicate further, as in the creation of the world. To this I say that the Son is the adequate communication of the Father's goodness, and is an express and complete image of Him. But the Son also has an inclination to communicate Himself in an image of His person that may partake of His happiness, and this was the end of the creation: even the communication of the happiness of the Son of God and this was the only motive herein, even the Son's inclination to this. Man, the consciousness or perception of the creation, is the immediate subject of this. Therefore the church is said to be the completeness of Christ (Ephesians 1:23), as if Christ were not complete without the church, as having a natural inclination thereto. We are incomplete without that which we have a natural inclination to. The man is incomplete without the woman: she is himself, as Christ is not complete without His spouse. The soul is not complete without the body, because human souls have a natural inclination to dwell in a body. See Ephesians 1 and 2, the last verses, and Proverbs 8:30–31. First we are told where the Father's delight was, and also the mutual delight of the Son, and then where the Son's delight is, in the object of His communication of his goodness. "Then I was by Him as one brought up with Him." The Son is the fullness of God, and the church is the fullness of the Son of God.

Then doubtless He is the only proper and fit person to be the Redeemer of men.

Therefore they are so nearly united to Christ and shall have such intimate communion with Him; they

shall sit down with Him on His throne, even as He is
set down on His Father's throne, and shall sit with Him
in the judgment of the world. And their glory and
honor and happiness shall be astonishingly great, as is
spoken of in the Scripture.

Therefore the Son created and governs the world,
seeing that the world was a communication of Him,
and seeing that the communication of His happiness is
the end of the world.

We may learn in what sense Christ says in John 15:9:
"As the Father loves the Son," as a communication of
Himself as begotten in pursuance of His eternal inclination to communicate Himself, so the Son of God
loves the church or the saints as the effect of His love
and goodness, and His natural inclination to communicate Himself.

Hence we find the meaning of Colossians 1:16–18.
In this verse there is a trinity, an image of the eternal
trinity, wherein Christ is the everlasting Father, believers are His seed, and the Holy Spirit, or Comforter, is
the third person in Christ, being His delight and love
flowing out towards the church. In believers, the Spirit
and delight of God is communicated unto them, flowing out towards the Lord Jesus Christ.

Hence we may plainly perceive how these
expressions of the Lord Jesus are to be understood in
John 17:21–24 and John 14:20. These sayings at first
seem like nothing but words carelessly cast together,
very abstruse and dark, but we may here see and know
what He meant. Many other of Christ's speeches may
receive light from hence; the meaning of the Apostle
John's gospel and epistles particularly, and many
passages through the whole Bible.

How glorious is the gospel that reveals to us such
things.

Hence we see why it is most suitable and proper that

the Son of God should have the immediate management of the affairs of the church, and that it should be this person of the Trinity who has all along manifested Himself by the visible tokens of His presence in the Antediluvians, the Patriarchs, and the Israelites.

But God the Father is not the object of creation, for the Father is not a communication of the Son, and therefore is not the object of the Son's goodness, but men—that is, those of them who are holy, as the Son says in Psalm 16:2–3. It is Christ here speaking, as is evident by the passage that follows.

God loves His creatures so, that He really loves the Being honored by them, as all try to be well thought of by those they love. Therefore, we are to seek the glory of God as that which is a thing really pleasing to Him.

It is indeed a decent thing that God should be the ultimate end of the creation as well as the cause, that in creating He should make Himself His end, that He should in this respect be Omega as well as Alpha. The Scripture says, "God hath made all things for Himself" (Proverbs 16:4); and this may be, and yet the reason for His creating the world can be His propensity to goodness, and the communication of happiness to creatures be the end. It was perhaps thus: God created the world for His Son that He might prepare for Him a spouse or bride to bestow His love upon, so that the mutual joys between this bride and bridegroom are the end of the creation. God is really happy in loving His creatures, because in so doing He glorifies a natural propensity in the divine nature, goodness. Yea, and He is really delighted in the love of His creatures, and in their glorifying Him, because He loves them, not because He needs them. For He could not be happy therein were it not for His love and goodness. Colossians 1:16: "All things were made by Him and for Him," that is, for the Son.

When God is said to make all things for Himself, no

more is necessarily understood by it than that He made all things for His own designs and purposes, and to put them to His own use. It is as much as to say that everything that is, everything that comes to pass, is altogether of God's ordering, and God has some design in it. It is for something that God aims at and will have obtained that this or the other thing is or happens, whatever it is, even sin and wickedness itself. It comes to pass because God has a use for it, a design and purpose to accomplish by it. Things do not happen merely to fulfill the desires or designs of some other being, some adversary of God. But all that is or comes to pass is of God's will and for His pleasure, and for His ends; it is not primarily of the will of some others and for their purposes, for then we are taught nothing by those words "for Himself." When it is said that God has made all things, that would have implied as much as that God made them for His own ends; for if God made things designedly it must be for some end.

There are many of the divine attributes that, if God had not created the world, never would have had any exercise: the power of God, the wisdom of God, the prudence and contrivance of God, the goodness, mercy and grace of God, and the justice of God. It is fitting that the divine attributes should have exercise. Indeed, God knew as perfectly that there were those attributes fundamentally in Himself before they were in exercise as since. But God, since He delights in His own excellency and glorious perfections, so He delights in the exercise of those perfections. It is true that there was from eternity that act in God, within Himself and towards Himself, that was the exercise of the same perfections of His nature. But it was not the same kind of exercise. It virtually contained it, but was not explicitly the same exercise of His perfection. God, who delights in the exercise of His own perfection, delights in all the kinds of its exercise.

For God to glorify Himself is to manifest Himself in His works, or to communicate Himself in His works, which is all one. Remember that the world exists only mentally, so that the very being of the world implies its being perceived or discovered. For God to glorify Himself is in His acts *ad extra* to act worthy of Himself, or to act excellently. Therefore, God does not seek His own glory because it makes Him happier to be honored and highly thought of, but because He loves to see Himself, His own excellencies and glories, appearing in His works. He loves to see Himself communicated, and it was His intention to communicate Himself that was a prime motive of His creating the world. His own glory was the ultimate motive. He Himself was His end, that is, Himself communicated. The very phrase "the glory" seems naturally to signify this. Glory is a shining forth, an effulgence. So the glory of God is the shining forth or effulgence of His perfections, or the communication of His perfections, as effulgence is the communication of light. For this reason, that brightness whereby God was wont to manifest Himself in the wilderness, and in the tabernacle and temple, was called God's glory. As the brightness of the sun, moon, and stars is called their glory, so the glory of God is the shining forth of His perfections. The world was created that they might shine forth, that is, that they might be communicated.

The Wisdom of God
Displayed in the Way of Salvation

"To the intent that now unto the principalities and powers in heavenly places might be known by the church the manifold wisdom of God." Ephesians 3:10

The wisdom appearing in the way of salvation by Jesus Christ is far above the wisdom of the angels. The apostle is speaking in the context of the glorious doctrine of the redemption of sinners by Jesus Christ, and how it was in a great measure kept hidden in the past ages of the world. It was a mystery that before they did not understand, but now it was in a glorious manner brought to light. Verses 3–5: "By revelation He made known unto me the mystery (as I wrote afore in few words; whereby when ye read ye may understand my knowledge in the mystery of Christ), which in other ages was not made known unto the sons of men, as it is now revealed unto His holy apostles and prophets by the Spirit." And verses 8–9: "Unto me, who am less than the least of all saints, is this grace given, that I should preach among the Gentiles the unsearchable riches of Christ; and to make all men see what is the fellowship of the mystery, which, from the beginning of the world, has been hid in God, who created all things by Jesus Christ."

The apostle in the text informs us that what Christ had accomplished towards His church, the work of redemption, had not only in a great measure unveiled the mystery to the church in this world, but God had more clearly and fully opened it to the understanding even of the angels themselves, and that this was one end of

God in it, to display the glory of His wisdom to the angels. "To the intent that now unto the principalities and powers in heavenly places might be known by the church the manifold wisdom of God."

One end of revealing God's counsels concerning the work of redemption is making known God's wisdom. It is called "manifold wisdom" because of the manifold glorious ends that are attained by it. The excellent designs hereby accomplished are very manifold. The wisdom of God in this is of vast extent. The contrivance is so manifold that one may spend an eternity in discovering more of the excellent ends and designs accomplished by it, and the multitude and vast variety of things that are, by divine contrivance, brought to conspire to the bringing about those ends.

We may observe to whom it is that God would manifest His wisdom by revealing the mystery of our redemption: not only men, but the angels. "To the intent that now unto the principalities and powers in heavenly places might be known the manifold wisdom of God." The angels are often called principalities and powers because of the exalted dignity of their nature. The angels excel in strength and wisdom. Those who are the wise men of the earth are called princes in the style of the apostle. 1 Corinthians 2:6: "Howbeit we speak wisdom among them that are perfect, yet not the wisdom of this world, nor of the princes of this world." Verse 8: "Which none of the princes of this world knew; for had they known it, they would not have crucified the Lord of glory." So the angels are called principalities for their great wisdom. They may also be so called for the honor God has put upon them in employing them as His ministers and instruments wherewith He governs the world, and therefore are called "thrones, dominions, principalities, and powers" in Colossians 1:16.

They are called "principalities and powers in heavenly places," to distinguish them from those who are in places of earthy power and dignity. The offices or places of dignity and power that the angels sustain are not earthly, but heavenly. They are places of honor and power in the heavenly city and the heavenly kingdom.

One end of God in revealing His design or contrivance for redemption, as He has so fully and gloriously done by Jesus Christ, is that the angels in heaven may behold the glory of His wisdom by it. Though they are such bright intelligences, and always behold the face of God the Father, and know so much, yet here is matter of instruction for them. Here they may see more of the diving wisdom than ever they had seen before. It was a new manifestation of the wisdom of God to them.

The time when this display of the wisdom of God was especially made to the angels is when Christ introduced the gospel dispensation, implied in those words: "To the intent that now unto the principalities." When Christ came into the world and died, and actually performed the work of redemption—when He had fully and plainly revealed the counsels of God concerning it, and accordingly introduced the evangelical dispensation, and erected the gospel church—then the angels understood more of the mystery of man's redemption, and the manifold designs and counsels of divine wisdom than ever they had done before.

In the foregoing verse the apostle, after speaking of revealing this wisdom of God to man ("And to make all men see what is the fellowship of this mystery"), speaks of this mystery as a thing from the beginning kept hidden till now. "The mystery which, from the beginning of the world, had been hid in God . . . that now," and so on. In this verse he mentions another end of God's, that He may at the same time make the angels also see God's wisdom in His glorious scheme of redemption. "Now at this time" implies that it was before a mystery kept hidden from them in comparison of what it is now. And here is room enough for the angels to discover more and more to all eternity of the wisdom of God in this work.

Observe the medium by which the angels come by this knowledge: the church. "That now unto principalities . . . might be known by the church," that is, by the things they see done in the church or towards the church, and by what they see concerning the church. So has it pleased the sovereign God that the angels should have the most glorious discoveries of divine wisdom by His doings towards His church, a sort of beings much inferior to themselves. It has pleased God to put this honor upon us.

The wisdom appearing in the way of salvation by Jesus Christ is far above the wisdom of the angels. For here it is mentioned as one end of God in revealing the contrivance of our salvation, that the angels thereby might see and know how great and manifold the wisdom of God is, to hold forth the divine wisdom to the angels' view and admiration. But why is it so, if this wisdom is not higher than their own wisdom? It never would have been mentioned as one end of revealing the contrivance of redemption, that the angels might see how manifold God's wisdom is, if all the wisdom to be seen in it was no greater than their own. It is mentioned as a wisdom such as they had never seen before, not in God, much less in themselves. That now might be known how manifold the wisdom of God is, now, four thousand years since the creation. In all that time the angels had always beheld the face of God, and had been studying God's works of creation. Yet they never, till that day, had seen anything like that; they never knew how manifold God's wisdom is as now they knew it by the church.

SECTION 1
Wonderful things done by which salvation is procured

1. Consider the choice of the person to be our redeemer. When God designed the redemption of mankind, His great wisdom appears in that He pitched upon His own, His only begotten Son, to be the person to perform the work. He was a redeemer of God's own choosing, and therefore He is called in Scripture "God's elect" (Isaiah 42:1). The wisdom of choosing this person to be the redeemer appears in His being in every way a fit person for this undertaking. It was necessary that the person who is the redeemer should be a divine person. None but a divine person was sufficient for this great work. The work is infinitely unequal to any creature. It was requisite that the redeemer of sinners should be Himself infinitely holy. None could take away the infinite evil of sin but one who was infinitely far from and contrary to sin Himself. Christ is a fit person upon this account.

It was requisite that the person, in order to be sufficient for this undertaking, should be one of infinite dignity and worthiness, so that He might be capable of meriting infinite blessings. The Son of God is a fit person on this account. It was necessary that He should be a person of infinite power and wisdom. For this work is so difficult that it requires such a one. Christ is a fit person also upon this account. It was requisite that He should be a person who was infinitely dear to God the Father in order to give an infinite value to His transactions in the Father's esteem, and that the Father's love for Him might balance the offense and provocation done by our sins. Christ is a fit person upon this account. Therefore He is called "the Beloved." Ephesians 1:6: "He has made us accepted in the Beloved."

It was requisite that the person should be one who could act in this of His own absolute right, one who, in Himself, is not a servant or subject. Because(if He is one who cannot act of His own right, He cannot merit anything.) He who is a servant, and who can do no more than he is bound to do, cannot merit. And then he who has nothing that is absolutely his own cannot pay any price to redeem another. Upon this account Christ is a fit person. And none but a divine person can be fit. He must also be a person of infinite mercy and love. For no other person but such a one would undertake a work so difficult for a creature so unworthy as man. Upon this account also Christ is a fit person. It was requisite that he should be a person of unchangeable perfect truth and faithfulness. Otherwise he would not be fit to be depended on by us in so great an affair. Christ is also a fit person upon this account.

The wisdom of God in choosing His eternal Son appears not only in that He is a fit person, but in that He was the only fit person of all persons, whether created or uncreated. No created person, neither man nor angel, was fit for this undertaking. For we have just now shown that He must be a person of infinite holiness, dignity, power, wisdom, and infinitely dear to God, one of infinite love and mercy, and one who may act of His own absolute right. But no creature, however excellent, has any one of these qualifications. There are three uncreated persons in the Trinity: the Father, the Son, and the Holy Ghost. And Christ alone of these was a suitable person for a redeemer.(It was not fitting that the redeemer should be God the Father because He, in the divine economy of the persons of the Trinity, was the person who holds the rights of the Godhead, and so was the person offended, whose justice required satisfaction, and was to be appeased by a mediator.) It was not fitting that it should be the Holy Ghost, for in be-

ing Mediator between the Father and the saints He is
in some sense so between the Father and the Spirit.
The saints, in all their spiritual transactions with God,
act by the Spirit; or rather, it is the Spirit of God that
acts in them. They are the temples of the Holy Ghost.
The Holy Spirit dwelling in them is their principle of
action in all their transactings with God. But in these
spiritual transactings with God, they act by a mediator.
These spiritual and holy exercises cannot be accept-
able, or avail anything with God, as from a fallen creature, but by a mediator. Therefore Christ, in being
Mediator between the Father and the saints, may be
said to be Mediator between the Father and the Holy
Spirit, who acts in the saints. And therefore it was fitting that the mediator should not be either the Father
or the Spirit, but a middle person between them both. It
is the Spirit in the saints who seeks the blessing of God
by faith and prayer, and, as the apostle says, with groanings that cannot be uttered. Romans 8:26: "Likewise the
Spirit also helpeth our infirmities: for we know not
what we should pray for as we ought; but the Spirit itself
maketh intercession for us, with groanings that cannot
be uttered." The Spirit in the saints seeks divine blessings from God by and through a mediator. And therefore that mediator must not be the Spirit, but another
person.

It shows a divine wisdom to know that He was a fit
person. None other but one of divine wisdom could
have known it. None but one of infinite wisdom could
have thought of Him to be a redeemer of sinners. For
He, since He is God, is one of the persons offended by
sin, against whom man by his sin had rebelled. Who
but God infinitely wise could ever have thought of Him
to be a redeemer of sinners, against whom they had
sinned, to whom they were enemies, and of whom they
deserved infinitely ill? Who would ever have thought of

Him as one who should set His heart upon man, and exercise infinite love and pity to him, and exhibit infinite wisdom, power, and merit in redeeming him?

2. Consider the substituting of this person in our place. After choosing the person to be our redeemer, the next step of divine wisdom is to contrive the way how He should perform this work. If God had declared who the person was who should do this work and had gone no further, no creature could have thought which way this person could have performed the work. If God had told them that His own Son must be the redeemer, that He alone was a fit person for the work, and that He was a person who was in every way fit and sufficient for it, but had proposed to them to contrive a way how this fit and sufficient person should proceed, we may well suppose that all created understandings would have been utterly at a loss.

The first thing necessary to be done is that this Son of God should become our representative and surety, and so be substituted in the sinner's place. But who of created intelligences would have thought of any such thing as the eternal and infinitely beloved Son of God being substituted in the place of sinners, His standing in stead of a sinner, a rebel, an object of the wrath of God? Who would have thought of a person of infinite glory representing sinful worms who had made themselves by sin infinitely provoking and abominable?

For if the Son of God is substituted in the sinner's place, then his sin must be charged upon Him. He will thereby take the guilt of the sinner upon Himself. He must be subject to the same law that man was, both as to the commands and threatenings. But who would have thought of any such thing concerning the Son of God?

3. Consider the incarnation of Jesus Christ. The next step of divine wisdom in contriving how Christ

should perform the work of redeeming sinners was in determining His incarnation. Suppose that God had revealed His counsels thus far to created understandings, that His own Son was the person chosen for this work, that He had substituted Him in the sinner's obligations and guilt on Himself, and had revealed no more, but had left the rest to them to find out. It is in no way probable that even then they could ever have thought of a way whereby this person might actually have performed the work of redemption. For if the Son of God is substituted in the sinner's stead, then He takes the sinner's obligations on Himself. For instance, He must take the obligation the sinner is under to perform perfect obedience to the divine law. But it is not probable that any creature could have conceived how that could be possible. How could a person who is the eternal JEHOVAH become a servant, be under law, and perform obedience to the law of man?

Again, if the Son of God is substituted in the sinner's stead, then He comes under the sinner's obligation to suffer the punishment which man's sin had deserved. And who could have thought that to be possible? For how could a divine person, who is essentially, unchangeably, and infinitely happy, suffer pain and torment? And how could He who is the object of God's infinitely dear love suffer the wrath of His Father? It is not to be supposed that created wisdom ever would have found out a way how to get over these difficulties. But divine wisdom has found out a way by the incarnation of the Son of God. The Word should be made flesh so that He might be both God and man in one person. What created understanding could have conceived that such a thing was possible? Yet these things could never be proved to be impossible. This distinction duly considered will show the futility of many Socinian objections.

And if God had revealed to them that it was possible and even that it should be, but left them to find out how it should be, we may well suppose that they would all have been puzzled and confounded to conceive of a way for so uniting a man to the eternal Son of God, that they should be but one person, that one who is truly a man in all respects, should indeed be the very same Son of God that was with God from all eternity. This is a great mystery to us. Hereby, a person that is infinite, omnipotent, and unchangeable, is become, in a sense, a finite, a feeble man, a man subject to our sinless infirmities, passions, and calamities! The great God, the sovereign of heaven and earth, is thus become a worm of the dust. Psalm 22:6: "I am a worm, and no man." He that is eternal and self-existent, and all-sufficient, now is come to stand in need of food and clothing. He becomes poor, "has not where to lay his head"—stands in need of the charity of men, and is maintained by it! It is far above us to conceive how it is done. It is a great wonder and mystery to us. But it was no mystery to divine wisdom.

4. Consider the life of Christ in this world. First, the wisdom of God appears in the circumstances of His life. If God had revealed that His own Son should be incarnate, and should live in this world in a human nature, and it was left to men to determine what circumstances of life would have been most suitable for Him, human wisdom would have determined that He would appear in the world in a most magnificent manner, with very extraordinary outward ensigns of honor, authority, and power, far above any of the kings of the earth. They would have determined that He would reign in great visible pomp and splendor over all nations. Thus men's wisdom determined before Christ came. The wise, the great men among the Jews, scribes and Pharisees, who are called "princes of this world," expected that the

Messiah would thus appear. But the wisdom of God chose quite otherwise. It chose that when the Son of God became man, He would begin His life in a stable, for many years dwell obscurely in a family of low degree in the world, and be in low outward circumstances; that He should be poor, and have nowhere to lay His head; that He should be maintained by the charity of some of His disciples; that He should "grow up as a tender plant, and as a root out of a dry ground" (Isaiah 53:2); "that He should not cry, nor lift up, nor cause His voice to be heard in the streets" (Isaiah 42:2); that He should come to Zion in a lowly manner, "riding on an ass, and a colt the foal of an ass"; that He should be "despised and rejected of men, a man of sorrows, and acquainted with grief."

And now that the divine determination in this matter is made known, we may safely conclude that it is by far the most suitable, and that it would not have been at all suitable for God, when He was manifest in flesh, to appear with earthly pomp, wealth, and grandeur. No! These things are infinitely too mean and despicable for the Son of God to show as if He affected or esteemed them. Men, if they had this way proposed to them, would have been ready to condemn it as foolish and very unsuitable for the Son of God. "But the foolishness of God is wiser than men" (1 Corinthians 1:25). And "God hath brought to nought the wisdom of this world, and the princes of this world" (1 Corinthians 2:6). Christ, by thus appearing in mean and low outward circumstances in the world, has poured contempt upon all worldly wealth and glory, and has taught us to despise it. And if it becomes mean men to despise them, how much more did it become the Son of God! And then Christ hereby has taught us to be lowly in heart. If He who was infinitely high and great was thus lowly, how lowly should we be, who are indeed so vile!

Second, the wisdom of God appears in the work and business of the life of Christ, particularly, that He should perfectly obey the law of God under such great temptations; that He should have conflicts with, and overcome for us in a way of obedience, the powers of earth and hell; that He should be subject to not only the moral law, but the ceremonial also, that heavy yoke of bondage. Christ went through the time of His public ministry delivering to us divine instructions and doctrines. The wisdom of God appears in giving us such a one to be our prophet and teacher who is a divine person, who is Himself the very wisdom and Word of God, and was from all eternity in the bosom of the Father. His word is of greater authority and weight than if delivered by the mouth of an ordinary prophet. And how wisely was it ordered that the same should be our Teacher and Redeemer, in order that His relations and offices as Redeemer might the more sweeten and endear His instructions to us. We are ready to give heed to what is said by those who are dear to us. Our love to their persons makes us to delight in their discourse. It is therefore wisely ordered that He who has done so much to endear Himself to us should be appointed to be our great Prophet, to deliver to us divine doctrines.

5. Consider the death of Christ. This is a means of salvation for poor sinners that none other than divine wisdom would have pitched upon. And when revealed, it was doubtless greatly to the surprise of all the hosts of heaven, and they never will cease to wonder at it. How astonishing is it that a person who is blessed forever, and is infinitely and essentially happy, should endure the greatest sufferings that ever were endured on earth; that a person who is the supreme Lord and Judge of the world should be arraigned, and should stand at the judgment seat of mortal worms, and then be condemned; that a person who is the living God, and the

Fountain of life, should be put to death; that a person who created the world and gives life to all His creatures should be put to death by His own creatures; that a person of infinite majesty and glory—and so the object of love, praises, and adorations of angels—should be mocked and spat upon by the vilest of men; that a person, infinitely good, and who is love itself, should suffer the greatest cruelty; that a person who is infinitely beloved of the Father should be put to inexpressible anguish under His own Father's wrath; that He who is King of heaven, who has heaven for His throne and the earth for His footstool, should be buried in the prison of the grave! How wonderful is this! And yet this is the way that God's wisdom has fixed upon as the way of a sinner's salvation, as being neither unsuitable nor dishonorable to Christ.

6. The last thing done to consider is Christ's exaltation. Divine wisdom saw it needful, or most expedient, that the same person who died upon the cross should sit at His right hand, on His own throne, as supreme Governor of the world, and should have particularly the absolute disposal of all things relating to man's salvation, and should be the Judge of the world. This was needful because it was requisite that the same person who purchased salvation bestow it. For it is not fitting that God should at all transact with the fallen creature in a way of mercy, but by a mediator. And this is exceedingly to strengthen the faith and comfort of the saints, that He who has endured so much to purchase salvation for them has all things in heaven delivered unto Him that He might bestow eternal life on them for whom he purchased it. And the same person who loved them so greatly as to shed His precious blood for them was to be their final Judge.

This then was another thing full of wonders, that He who was man as well as God, He who was a servant and died like a malefactor, should be made the sovereign Lord of heaven and earth, angels and men, the absolute disposer of eternal life and death, the supreme Judge of all created intelligent beings, for eternity, and should have committed to Him all the governing power of God the Father—and that not only as God, but as God-man, not exclusive of the human nature.

As it is wonderful that a person who is truly divine should be humbled so as to become a servant, and to suffer as a malefactor, so it is in like manner wonderful that He who is God-man, not exclusive of the manhood, should be exalted to the power and honor of the great God of heaven and earth. But such wonders as these has infinite wisdom contrived, and accomplished in order to our salvation.

SECTION 2
In this way of salvation God is greatly glorified

God has greatly glorified Himself in the work of creation and providence. All His works praise Him, and His glory shines brightly from them all. But as some stars differ from others in glory, so the glory of God shines brighter in some of His works than in others. And among all these, the work of redemption is like the sun in its strength. The glory of the Author is abundantly the most resplendent in this work.

1. Each attribute of God is glorified in the work or redemption. How God has exceedingly glorified His wisdom may more fully appear before we have done with this subject.

But more particularly, first, God has exceedingly glorified His power in this work. It shows the great and inconceivable power of God to unite natures so infinitely different as the divine and human nature in one person. If God can make one who is truly God and one who is truly man the self-same person, what is it that He cannot do? This is a greater and more marvelous work than creation.)

The power of God most gloriously appears in man's being actually saved and redeemed in this way, in his being brought out of a state of sin and misery into a conformity to God, and at last to the full and perfect enjoyment of God. This is a more glorious demonstration of divine power than creating things out of nothing, and that upon two accounts. One is, the effect is greater and more excellent. To produce the new creature is a more glorious effect than merely to produce a creature. Making a holy creature, a creature in the spiritual image of God, in the image of the divine excellencies, and a partaker of the divine nature, is a greater effect than merely to give being. And therefore, since the effect is greater, it is a more glorious manifestation of power.

And then, in this effect of the actual redemption of sinners, the term *from* which is more distant from the term *to* which than in the work of creation. The term from which, in the work of creation, is nothing, and the term to which is being. But the term from which, in the work of redemption, is a state infinitely worse than nothing; and the term to which, a holy and a happy being, a state infinitely better than mere being. The terms in the production of the last are much more remote from one another than in the first.

And then the production of this last effect is a more glorious manifestation of power than the work of creation, the terms are very distant—as "nothing" is very remote from "being"—yet there is no opposition to the creating power of God. But in redemption, the divine power meets with and overcomes great opposition. There is great opposition in a state of sin to a state of grace. Men's lusts and corruptions are exceedingly opposite to grace and holiness, and greatly resist the production of the effect. But this opposition is completely overcome in actual redemption.

Besides, there is great opposition from Satan. The power of God is very glorious in this work because it therein conquers the strongest and most powerful enemies. Power never appears more illustrious than in conquering. Jesus Christ, in this work, conquers and triumphs over thousands of devils, strong and mighty spirits, uniting all their strength against Him. Luke 11:21: "When a strong man armed keepeth his palace, his goods are in peace; but when a stronger than he shall overcome him, he taketh from him all his armor wherein he trusted, and divideth his spoil." Colossians 2:15: "And having spoiled principalities and powers, He made a show of them openly, triumphing over them in the cross."

Second, the justice of God is exceedingly glorified in this work. God is so strictly and immutably just that He would not spare His beloved Son when He took upon Him the guilt of men's sins, and was substituted in the place of sinners. He would not abate Him the least mite of that debt which justice demanded. Justice should take place though it cost His infinitely dear Son His precious blood, and His enduring such extraordinary reproach, pain, and death in its most dreadful form.

Third, the holiness of God is also exceedingly glorious in this work. Never did God so manifest His hatred of sin as in the death and sufferings of His only begotten Son. Hereby He showed himself unappeasable to sin, and that it was impossible for Him to be at peace with it.

Fourth, God has also exceedingly glorified His truth in both His threatenings and promises. Herein is fulfilled the threatenings of the law, wherein God said, "In the day thou eatest thereof, thou shalt surely die. And cursed is every one that continueth not in all things written in the book of the law to do them." God showed hereby that not only heaven and earth should pass away, but, which is more, that the blood of Him who is the eternal Jehovah should be spilled rather than one jot or tittle of His Word should fail, till all is fulfilled.

Fifth, and last, God has exceedingly glorified His mercy and love in this work. The mercy of God was an attribute never seen before in its exercises till it was seen in this work of redemption, or the fruits of it. The goodness of God appeared towards the angels in giving them being and blessedness. It appeared glorious towards man in his primitive state, a state of holiness and happiness. But now God has shown that He can find it in His heart to love sinners, who deserve His infinite hatred; and not only has He shown that He can love them, but love them so as to give them more and do greater things for them than ever He did for the holy angels, who never sinned or offended their Creator. He loved sinful men so as to give them a greater gift than ever He gave the angels; so as to give His own Son, and not only to give Him to be their possession and enjoyment, but to give Him to be their sacrifice. And herein He has done more for them than if He had given them all the visible world, yea, more than if He had given them all the angels, and all heaven besides. God has loved them so much that hereby He purchased for them deliverance from eternal misery and the possession of immortal glory.

2. Each person of the Trinity is exceedingly glorified in this work. Herein the work of redemption is distinguished from all the other works of God. The attributes of God are glorious in His other works. But the three persons of the Trinity are distinctly glorified in

no work as in this of redemption. In this work every distinct person has His distinct parts and offices assigned to Him. Each one has His particular and distinct concern in it, agreeable to their distinct, personal properties, relations, and economic offices. The redeemed have an equal concern with and dependence upon each person in this affair, and owe equal honor and praise to each of them.

The Father appoints and provides the Redeemer, and accepts the price of redemption. The Son is the Redeemer and the price. He redeems by offering up Himself. The Holy Ghost immediately communicates to us the thing purchased. Yea, and He is the good purchased. The sum of what Christ purchased for us is holiness and happiness. But the Holy Ghost is the great principle both of all holiness and happiness. The Holy Ghost is the sum of all that Christ purchased for men. Galatians 3:13–14: "He was made a curse for us, that we might receive the promise of the Spirit through faith."

The blessedness of the redeemed consists in partaking of Christ's fullness, which consists in partaking of that Spirit which is given not by measure unto Him. This is the oil that was poured upon the head of the church, which ran down to the members of His body to the skirts of His garment. Thus we have an equal concern with and dependence upon each of the persons of the Trinity distinctly: upon the Father, as He provides the Redeemer, and the person of whom the purchase is made; the Son as the purchaser and the price; the Holy Ghost as the good purchased.

SECTION 3
*The good attained by salvation is wonderfully
various and exceedingly great*

Here we may distinctly consider the variety and the
greatness of the good procured for men.

1. The good procured by salvation is wonderfully
various. Here all sorts of good are procured for fallen
man that he does or can really need, or is capable of.
The wisdom of God appears in the way of salvation in
that it is most worthy of an infinitely wise God because
it is in every way perfect and sufficient. We, in our fallen
state, are most needy creatures, full of wants; but they
are here all answered. Every sort of good is here procured, whatever would really contribute to our happiness, and even many things that we could not have
thought of, had not Christ purchased them for us, and
revealed them to us. Every demand of our circumstances, and craving of our natures, is here exactly answered.

For instance, first, we stand in need of peace with
God. We had provoked God to anger. His wrath abode
upon us, and we needed to have it appeased. This is
done for us in this way of salvation. For Christ, by shedding His blood, has fully satisfied justice and appeased
God's wrath for all who shall believe in Him. By the
sentence of the law we were condemned to hell. And we
needed to have our sins pardoned that we might be delivered from hell. But in this work, pardon of sin and
deliverance from hell is fully purchased for us.

Second, we needed not only to have God's wrath appeased and our sins pardoned, but we needed to have
the favor of God; to have God not only not be our enemy, but be our friend. Now God's favor is purchased
for us by the righteousness of Jesus Christ.

Third, we needed not only to be delivered from hell, but to have some satisfying happiness bestowed. Man has a natural craving and thirst after happiness. And he will thirst and crave till his capacity is filled, a capacity of vast extent. And nothing but an infinite good can fill and satisfy his desires. But, notwithstanding, provision is made in this way of salvation to answer those needs; there is a satisfying happiness purchased for us, that which is fully answerable to the capacity and cravings our souls.

Here is food procured to answer all the appetites and faculties of our souls. God has made the soul of man of a spiritual nature. And therefore he needs a corresponding happiness, some spiritual object, in the enjoyment of which he may be happy. Christ has purchased the enjoyment of God, who is the great and original Spirit, as the portion of our souls. And He has purchased the Spirit of God to come and dwell in us as an eternal principle of happiness.

God has made man a rational, intelligent creature. And man needs some good that shall be a suitable object of his understanding for him to contemplate, wherein he may have full and sufficient exercise for his capacious faculties in their utmost extent. Here is an object that is great and noble, and worthy of the exercise of the noblest faculties of the rational soul. God Himself should be theirs, for them forever to behold and contemplate. His glorious perfections and works are most worthy objects. And there is room enough for improving them, and still to exercise their faculties to all eternity. What object can be more worthy to exercise the understanding of a rational soul than the glories of the Divine Being, with which the heavenly intelligences, and even the infinite understanding of God Himself is entertained.

Our souls need some good that shall be a suitable

object of the will and affections, a suitable object for
the choice, the acquiescence, the love, and the joy of
the rational soul. Provision is made for this also in this
way of salvation. There is an infinitely excellent Being
offered to be chosen, to be rested in, to be loved, to be
rejoiced in, by us, even God Himself, who is infinitely
lovely, the fountain of all good; a fountain that can
never be exhausted, where we can be in no danger of
going to excess in our love and joy. And here we may be
assured ever to find our joy and delight in enjoyments
answerable to our love and desires.

Fourth, there is all possible enjoyment of this object
procured in this way of salvation. When persons entirely set their love upon another, they naturally desire
to see that person. Merely to hear of the person does
not satisfy love. So here is provision made that we
should see God, the object of our supreme love. Not
only that we should hear and read of Him in His Word,
but that we should see Him with a spiritual eye here.
And not only so, but that we should have the satisfaction of seeing God face to face hereafter. This is
promised in Matthew 5:8: "Blessed are the pure in
heart, for they shall see God." It is promised that we
shall not see God as through a glass darkly, as we do
now, but face to face (1 Corinthians 13:12), that we shall
see Christ as He is (1 John 3:2).

We naturally desire not only to see those whom we
love, but to converse with them. Provision is made for
this also, that we should have spiritual conversation
with God while in this world, and that we should be
hereafter admitted to converse with Christ in the most
intimate manner possible. Provision is made in this
way of salvation, that we should converse with God
much more intimately than otherwise it would have
been possible for us. For now Christ is incarnate, is in
our nature. He has become one of us, whereby we are

under advantages for an immensely more free and intimate converse with Him than could have been if He had remained only in the divine nature, and so in a nature infinitely distant from us. We naturally desire not only to converse with those whom we greatly love, but to dwell with them. Provision, through Christ, is made for this. It is purchased and provided that we should dwell with God in His own house in heaven, which is called our Father's house, to dwell forever in God's presence, and at His right hand.

We naturally desire to have a right in that person whom we greatly love. Provision is made in this way of salvation that we should have a right in God, a right to Him. This is the promise of the covenant of grace, that He will be our God. God, with all His glorious perfections and attributes, with all His power and wisdom, and with all His majesty and glory, will be ours. So we may call Him our inheritance, and the portion of our souls. What we can humbly claim by faith is having this portion made over to us by a firm instrument, by a covenant ordered in all things and sure. And we may also hereby claim a right to Jesus Christ. Love desires that the right should be mutual. The lover desires not only to have a right to the beloved, but that the beloved should also have a right to him. He desires to be his beloved's, as well as his beloved should be his. Provision is also made for this in this wise method of salvation, that God should have a special propriety in the redeemed, that they should be in a distinguishing manner His, that they should be His peculiar people. We are told that God sets apart the godly for Himself (Psalm 4:3). They are called God's jewels. The spouse speaks it with great satisfaction and rejoicing in Song of Solomon 2:16, "My beloved is mine, and I am His."

Love desires to stand in some near relation to the beloved. Provision is made by Christ that we should stand in the nearest possible relation to God, that He should be our Father and we His children. We are often instructed in the Holy Scriptures that God is the Father of believers, and that they are His family; and not only so, but they stand in the nearest relation to Christ Jesus. There is the closest union possible. The souls of believers are married to Christ. The church is the bride, the Lamb's wife. Yea, there is yet a nearer similitude. Believers are as the very members of Christ, His flesh and His bones (Ephesians 5:30). Yea, this is not near enough yet, but they are one spirit (1 Corinthians 6:17).

Love naturally inclines to a conformity to the beloved, to have those excellencies, upon the account of which he is beloved, copied in himself. Provision is made in this way of salvation that we may be conformed to God, that we shall be transformed into the same image. 2 Corinthians 3:18: "We all with open face, beholding as in a glass the glory of the Lord, are changed into the same image from glory to glory." And hereafter we shall see Him as He is and be like Him.

It is the natural desire of love to do something for the beloved, either for his pleasure or honor. Provision is made for this also in this way of salvation, that we should be made instruments of glorifying God, and promoting His kingdom here, and glorifying Him to all eternity.

Fifth, in this way of salvation, provision is made for our having every sort of good that man naturally craves, such as honor, wealth, and pleasure. Here provision is made that we should be brought to the highest honor. This is what God has promised, that those who honor Him, He will honor. And true Christians shall be kings and priests unto God. Christ promised that, as His Father has appointed unto Him a kingdom, so He will appoint unto them that they may eat and drink at His table in His kingdom. He has promised to crown them

with a crown of glory, and that they shall sit with Him
in His throne. He will confess their names before His
Father and before His angels. He will give them a new
name, and they shall walk with Him in white.

Christ has also purchased for them the greatest
wealth. All those who are in Christ are now rich. They
have the best riches, being rich in faith, and the graces
of the Spirit of God. They have gold tried in the fire.
They have durable riches and righteousness. They have
treasure in heaven, where neither thief approaches nor
moth corrupts. They have an inheritance that is incorruptible, undefiled, and does not fade away. They are
possessors of all things.

Christ has also purchased pleasure for them, pleasures that are immensely preferable to all the pleasures
of sense, most exquisitely sweet and satisfying. He has
purchased for them fullness of joy and pleasures
forevermore at God's right hand. And they shall drink
of the river of God's pleasure.

Sixth, Christ has purchased all needed good for
both soul and body. While we are here, we stand in
need of these earthly things. And of these Christ has
purchased all that are best for us. He has purchased for
the body that God should feed and clothe us. Matthew
6:26: "How much more shall He feed you, O ye of little
faith!" How much more shall He clothe you! Christ has
purchased, that God should take care of us, and provide
what is needed of these things, as a father provides for
his children. 1 Peter 5:7: "Casting your care upon Him,
for He careth for you."

Seventh, Christ has purchased good that is suitable
for His people in all conditions. There is in this way of
salvation respect had to and provision made for all circumstances that they can be in. Here is provision made
for a time of affliction, for a time of poverty and pinch-
ing want, for a time of bereavement and mourning, for

spiritual darkness, for a day of temptation, for a time of persecution, and for a time of death. Here is such a provision made that is sufficient to carry a person above death, and to give him a complete triumph over that king of terrors. Here is enough to sweeten the grave and make it cease to seem desirable, and in its near approach to be not terrible but joyful.

Eighth, there is provision made in this way of salvation for the life and blessedness of soul and body to all eternity. Christ has purchased that we should be delivered from a state of temporal death as well as spiritual and eternal. The bodies of the saints shall be raised to life. He has purchased all manner of perfection for the body of which it is capable. It shall be raised a spiritual body in incorruption and glory, and be made like Christ's glorious body, to shine as the sun in the kingdom of His Father, and to exist in a glorified state in union with the soul to all eternity.

Ninth, but man in his fallen state still needs something else in order to obtain his happiness that these forementioned blessings should be purchased for him: he needs to be qualified for the possession and enjoyment of them. In order to our having a title to these blessings of the covenant of grace (so that we can scripturally claim an interest in them), there is a certain condition that must be performed by us. We must believe in the Lord Jesus Christ, and accept Him as offered in the gospel for a Savior. But since we cannot do this by ourselves, Christ has purchased this also for all the elect. He has purchased that they shall have faith given them, whereby they shall be united to Christ, and so have a title to His benefits.

But still something further is necessary for man, in order to his coming to the actual possession of the inheritance. A man, as soon as he has believed, has a title to the inheritance. But in order to come to the actual possession of it, he must persevere in a way of holiness. There is not only a gate that must be entered, but there is a narrow way that must be traveled before we can arrive at heavenly blessedness. And that is a way of universal and persevering holiness. But men, after they have believed, cannot persevere in a way of holiness of themselves. But there is sufficient provision made for this also in the way of salvation by Jesus Christ. The matter of a saint's perseverance is sufficiently secured by the purchase that Christ has made.

But still there is something else needful in order to qualify a person for the actual entering upon the enjoyments and employments of a glorified estate: that he should be made perfectly holy, that all remainders of sin should be taken away. For there cannot any sin enter into heaven. No soul may go into the glorious presence of God, with the least degree of the filth of sin. But there is provision made, for Christ has purchased that all sin shall be taken away out of the hearts of believers at death, and that they should be made perfectly holy, whereby they shall be fully and perfectly qualified to enter upon the pleasures and enjoyments of the new Jerusalem.

2. Consider the good attained for us by this way of salvation as being exceedingly great. There is not only every sort of good we need, but of every sort in that degree, so as to answer the extent of our capacity, the greatest stretch of our desires, and indeed of our conceptions. They are not only greater than our conceptions are here, but also greater than ever they could be, were it not that God's relation, and our own experience, will teach us. They are greater than the tongue of angels can declare. The deliverance that we have in it is exceedingly great. It is deliverance from guilt, from sin itself, from the anger of God, and from the miseries of hell.

How great is the good conferred! The objective good is the infinite God and the glorious Redeemer, Jesus Christ. How great is the love of the Father and the Son! And how near the relationship is between them and the true believer! How close the union, how intimate the communion, and ultimately how clear will be the vision in glory!

There are great communications made to the believing soul on earth, but how much greater in heaven! Then their conformity to God will be perfect, their enjoyment of Him will be full, their honor great and unsullied, and the glory of body and soul ineffable. The riches of the Christian are immense. All things are included in his treasure. Pleasures unspeakably and inconceivably great await him, rivers of delight, fullness of joy, and all of infinite duration.

The benefit procured for us is doubly infinite. Our deliverance is an infinite benefit, because the evil we are delivered from is infinite. And the positive good bestowed is eternal, the full enjoyment of all those blessings merited.

SECTION 4
How angels are benefited by the salvation of men

The wisdom of God has contrived this affair so that the benefit of what He has done therein should be so extensive as to reach the elect angels. It is for men that the work of redemption is wrought out. And yet the benefit of the things done in this work is not confined to them, though all that is properly called redemption, or included in it, is confined to men. The angels cannot partake in this, having never fallen. Yet they have great indirect benefit by it. God has so wisely ordered that what has been done in this directly and especially for men should redound to the exceeding benefit of all intelligent creatures who are in favor with God. The benefit of it is so diffusive as to reach heaven itself. So great and manifold is the good attained in this work that those glorious spirits who are so much above us, and were so highly exalted in happiness before, yet should receive great addition hereby. I will show how in some particulars.

✓ 1. The angels hereby see a great and wonderful manifestation of the glory of God. The happiness of angels as well as of men consists very much in beholding the glory of God. The excellency of the Divine Being is a most delightful subject of contemplation to the saints on earth, but much more to the angels in heaven. The more holy any being is, the more sweet and delightful will it be to him to behold the glory and beauty of the Supreme Being. Therefore, beholding the glory of God must be ravishing to the holy angels of God who are perfect in holiness and never had their minds leavened with sin. The manifestations of the glory of God are, as it were, the food that satisfies the angels. They live thereon. It is their greatest happiness.

It is without doubt much of their employment to behold the glory of God appearing in His works. Therefore this work of redemption greatly contributes to their happiness and delight, since the glory of God is so exceedingly manifested by it. For what is done is done in the sight of the angels, as is evident by many passages of Holy Scripture. And they behold the glory of God appearing herein with entertainment and delight, as is manifest by 1 Peter 1:12: "Which things the angels desire to look into."

The angels have this advantage, that now they may behold the glory of God in the face of Jesus Christ, where it shines with a peculiar luster and brightness. 1 Timothy 3:16: "Great is the mystery of godliness. God was manifested in the flesh, justified in the spirit, seen of angels." Perhaps all God's attributes are more gloriously manifested in this work than in any other that ever the angels saw. There is certainly a fuller manifestation of some of His attributes than ever they saw before, as is evident by the text. And especially it is so with respect to the mercy of God, that sweet and endearing attribute of the divine nature. The angels of heaven never saw so much grace manifested before as in the work of redemption, nor in any measure equal to it. How full of joy does it fill the hearts of the angels to see such a boundless and bottomless ocean of love and grace in their God. And therefore, with what rejoicing do all the angels praise Christ for His being slain! Revelation 5:11–12: "And I beheld and heard the voice of many angels round about the throne, and the beasts and the elders; and the number of them was ten thousand times ten thousand, and thousands of thousands, saying with a loud voice, 'Worthy is the Lamb that was slain to receive power, and riches, and wisdom, and strength, and honor, and glory, and blessing.' "

2. They have this benefit by it, that hereby Jesus Christ, God-man, has become their Head. God, subsisting in three persons, Father, Son, and Holy Ghost, was the king of angels, and would have been, if it had not been for our redemption. But it was owing to what is done in this work that Jesus Christ as God-man becomes the head of the angels. Christ is now not only the head of angels simply as God, but as God-man. Colossians 2:10: "And ye are complete in Him, who is the head of all principality and power." Ephesians 1:20–22: "Which He wrought in Christ, when He raised Him from the dead, and set Him on His own right hand in heavenly places, far above all principality and power, and might and dominion, and every name that is named, not only in this world, but also in that which is

to come. And hath put all things under His feet, and gave Him to be head over all things to the church."

This is a part of the exaltation and glory of Christ which God confers on Him as His reward—and not only so, but it is greatly to the angels' benefit. It is God's manner in His dealings with His elect creatures, in the same works wherein He glorifies Himself or His Son, greatly to benefit them. The same dealings of His that are most for His glory shall be most for their good. That Christ, God-man, should be made the head of the angels is greatly to their benefit in several ways:

First, because they become hereby more nearly related to so glorious a person, the Son of God, than otherwise they would have been. The angels esteem it a great honor done them to be related to such a person as Jesus Christ, God-man, who is an infinitely honorable person.

The angels, by Christ becoming their head, are with the saints gathered together in one in Christ (Ephesians 1:10). They, by virtue hereof, though Christ is not their Redeemer as He is ours, have a right and propriety in this glorious person as well as we. (He is theirs; though not their Savior, yet He is their head of government, and head of influence.)

Second, this is greatly to their benefit, since they are under advantages for a far more intimate converse with God. The divine nature is at an infinite distance from the nature of angels as well as from the nature of man. This distance forbids a familiarity and intimacy of intercourse. It is therefore a great advantage to the angels that God has come to them in a created nature, and in that nature has become their head, so that their intercourse and enjoyment may be more intimate. They are invited by the similar qualifications of the created nature with which the Son of God is invested.

Third, it is for the benefit of the angels since hereby

the elect of mankind are gathered into their society. Christ, by the work of redemption, gathers in the elect of mankind to join the angels of heaven. Ephesians 1:10: "That in the dispensation of the fullness of times, He might gather in one all things in Christ, both which are in heaven, and which are on earth, even in Him." Men are brought in to join with the angels in their work of praising God, to partake with them of their enjoyments. The angels greatly rejoice at this. They rejoice when but one person is gathered in, as Christ teaches us in Luke 15:10: "Likewise I say unto you, there is joy in the presence of the angels of God over one sinner that repenteth." The heavenly society is made more complete by this accession of the saints to it. They contribute to the happiness of each other. The angels rejoice that others are added to join them and assist them in praising God. And thus the vacancy by the fall of angels is filled up.

Fourth, it tends to make the angels prize their happiness more when they see how much it cost to purchase the same happiness for man. Though they knew so much, yet they are not incapable of being taught more and more the worth of their own happiness. For when they saw how much it cost to purchase the same happiness for man, even the precious blood of the Son of God, this tended to give them a great sense of the infinite value of their happiness. They never saw such a testimony of the value of the eternal enjoyment of God before. Thus we have shown how the wisdom of God appears in the work of redemption in the good ends attained thereby, with respect to God, men, and good angels.

But are there any good ends obtained with respect to bad angels, God's grand enemies? Undoubtedly there are, as may appear from the few following considerations. Satan and his angels rebelled against God in heaven, and proudly presumed to try their strength with His. And when God, by His almighty power, overcame the strength of Satan, and sent him like lightning from heaven to hell with all his army, Satan still hoped to get the victory by subtlety. Though he could not overcome by power, yet he hoped to succeed by craft, and so by his subtlety to disappoint God of His end in creating this lower world. God therefore has shown His great wisdom in overthrowing Satan's design. He has disappointed the devices of the crafty so that they cannot perform their enterprise. He has carried their counsel headlong.

Satan thought to have disappointed God of His glory, which He designed in creation this lower world, and to make mankind be for his own glory, in setting up himself god over them. Now Christ, by what He has done in the work of redemption, has overthrown Satan, and utterly frustrated him as to this end. God is exceedingly glorified in the elect, to the surprise of angels and devils. God by redemption has all the glory that He intended, and more than either men, angels, or devils imagined that God intended. God might have glorified His justice in the destruction of all mankind. But it was God's design in creating the world to glorify His goodness and love; and not only to be glorified eventually, but to be served and glorified actually by men. Satan intended to frustrate God of this end. But, by the redemption of Jesus Christ, his design is confounded.

Another design of the devil was to gratify his envy in the utter destruction of mankind. But, by the redemption of Jesus Christ, this malicious design of Satan is crossed, because all the elect are brought to their designed happiness, which is much greater than ever Satan thought it was in God's heart to bestow on man. And though some of mankind are left to be miserable, yet that does not answer Satan's end. For this also is or-

dered for God's glory. No more are left miserable than
God saw meet to glorify His justice upon.

One end why God suffered Satan to do what he did
in procuring the fall of man was that His Son might be
glorified in conquering that strong, subtle, and proud
spirit, and triumphing over him. How glorious does
Christ Jesus appear in baffling and triumphing over
this proud king of darkness, and all the haughty con-
federate rulers of hell! How glorious a sight is it to see
the meek and patient Lamb of God leading that proud,
malicious, and mighty enemy in triumph! What songs
does this cause in heaven! It was a glorious sight in
Israel, who came out with timbrels and with dances,
and sang, "Saul hath slain his thousands, and David his
ten thousands." But how much more glorious to see the
Son of David, the Son of God, carrying the head of the
spiritual Goliath, the champion of the armies of hell,
in triumph to the heavenly Jerusalem! It is with a principal view to this that Christ is called "the Lord of
hosts, or armies, and a man of war" (Exodus 15:3). And
Psalm 24:8: "Who is this king of glory! The Lord strong
and mighty, the Lord mighty in battle."

SECTION 5
In this way of salvation wonderful glory redounds
to God, as to the effect of divine wisdom

1. By this contrivance for our redemption, God's
greatest dishonor is made an occasion of His greatest
glory. Sin is a thing by which God is greatly dishonored. The nature of its principle is enmity against God,
and contempt of Him. And man, by his rebellion, has
greatly dishonored God. But this dishonor, by the contrivance of our redemption, is made an occasion of the
greatest manifestation of God's glory that ever was. Sin,

the greatest evil, is made an occasion of the greatest
good. It is the nature of a principle of sin that it seeks
to dethrone God. But this is made an occasion of the
greatest manifestation of God's royal majesty and glory
that ever was. By sin, man has slighted and despised
God; but this is made an occasion of His appearing the
more greatly honorable. Sin casts contempt upon the
authority and law of God. But by the contrivance of our
redemption, this is made the occasion of the greatest
honor done to that same authority, and to that very law.
It was a greater honor to the law of God that Christ was
subject to it, and obeyed it, than if all mankind had
obeyed it. It was greater honor to God's authority that
Christ showed such great respect, and such entire sub-
jection to it, than the perfect obedience of all the angels in heaven. Man by his sin showed his enmity
against the holiness of God. But this is made an occasion of the greatest manifestation of God's holiness.
The holiness of God never appeared to so great a degree as when God executed vengeance upon His own
dear Son.

2. So has the wisdom of God contrived that those attributes are glorified in man's salvation whose glory
seemed to require his destruction. When man had
fallen, several attributes of God seemed to require his
destruction. The justice of God requires that sin be
punished as it deserves. But it deserves no less than
eternal destruction. God proclaims it as a part of glory
of His nature that He will in no wise clear the guilty
(Exodus 34:7). The holiness of God seemed to require
man's destruction. For God by His holiness infinitely
hates sin. This seemed to require therefore that God
should manifest a proportionable hatred of the sinner,
and that He should forever be an enemy unto him. The
truth of God seemed also to require man's destruction.
For eternal death was what God had threatened for sin,

one jot or tittle of which threatening cannot by any means pass away. But yet so has God contrived that those very attributes not only allow of man's redemption, and are not inconsistent with it, but they are glorified in it. Even vindictive justice is glorified in the death and sufferings of Christ. The holiness of God, or His holy hatred of sin, that seemed to require man's damnation, is seen in Christ's dying for sinners. So herein also is manifested and glorified the truth of God, in the threatenings of the law.

3. Yea, it is so ordered now that the glory of these attributes requires the salvation of those who believe. The justice of God that required man's damnation, and seemed inconsistent with his salvation, now as much requires the salvation of those who believe in Christ as ever before it required their damnation. Salvation is an absolute debt to the believer from God, so that he may in justice demand it on account of what his Surety has done. For Christ has satisfied justice fully for his sin. It is but a piece of justice that the creditor should release the debtor when he has fully paid the debt. And again, the believer may demand eternal life because it has been merited by Christ, by a merit of condignity. So is it contrived that the justice that seemed to require man's destruction now requires his salvation.

The truth of God that seemed to require man's damnation now requires his salvation. At the same time that the threatening of the law stands good, there is a promise of eternal life to many who have broken the law. They both stand good at the same time. And the truth of God requires that both should be fulfilled. However much they seemed to clash, yet so is the matter contrived in this way of salvation that both are fulfilled and do not interfere one with another.

At the very time that God uttered the threatening, "In the day thou eatest thereof thou shalt surely die,"

and at the time that Adam had first eaten the forbidden
fruit, there was then an existing promise that many
thousands of Adam's race should obtain eternal life.
This promise was made to Jesus Christ before the world
was. What a difficulty and inconsistency did there seem
to be here? But it was no difficulty to the wisdom of God
that the promise and the threatening should be both
fully accomplished to the glory of God's truth in each
of them. Psalm 85:10: "Mercy and truth are met together; righteousness and peace have kissed each
other."

4. Those very attributes which seemed to require
man's destruction are more glorious in his salvation
than they would have been in his destruction. The re-
venging justice of God is a great deal more manifested
in the death of Christ than it would have been if all
mankind had been sufferers to all eternity. If man had
remained under the guilt and imputation of sin, the
justice of God would not have had such a trial as it had
when His own Son was under the imputation of sin. If
all mankind had stood guilty, and justice had called for
vengeance upon them, that would not have been such a
trial of the inflexibleness and unchangeableness of the
justice of God as when His own Son, who was the object
of His infinite love, and in whom He infinitely delighted, stood with the imputation of guilt upon Him.

This was the greatest trial that could be to manifest
whether God's justice was perfect and unchangeable or
not, whether God was so just that He would not upon
any account abate what justice required, and whether
God would have any respect to persons in judgment.

So the majesty of God appears much more in the
sufferings of Christ than it would have done in the
eternal sufferings of all mankind. The majesty of a
prince appears greater in the just punishment of great
personages under the guilt of treason than of inferior

persons. The sufferings of Christ have this advantage over the eternal sufferings of the wicked, for impressing upon the minds of the spectators a sense of the dread majesty of God, and His infinite hatred of sin: that the eternal sufferings of the wicked never will be seen actually accomplished and finished, whereas they have seen that which is equivalent to those eternal sufferings actually fulfilled and finished in the sufferings of Christ.

5. Such is the wisdom of salvation that the more any of the elect have dishonored God, the more is God glorified in this redemption. Such wonders as these are accomplished by the wisdom of this way of salvation. Such things as these, if they had been proposed to any created intelligence, would have seemed strange and unaccountable paradoxes, till the counsels of divine wisdom concerning the matter were unfolded.

So sufficient is this way of salvation that it is not inconsistent with any of God's attributes to save the chief of sinners. However great a sinner any one has been, yet God can, if He pleased, save without any injury to the glory of any one attribute. And not only so, but the more sinful any one has been, the more God glorifies Himself in his salvation. Much more does He glorify His power that he can redeem one in whom sin so abounds, and of whom Satan has such strong possession. The greater triumph has Christ over his grand adversary in redeeming and setting at liberty from his bondage those who were his greatest vassals. The more does the sufficiency of Christ appear in that it is sufficient for such vile wretches.

The more is the sovereignty and boundless extent of the mercy of God manifested, in that it is sufficient to redeem those who are undeserving. Romans 5:20: "Where sin abounded, grace did much more abound."

SECTION 6

How the wisdom of God appears in the manner
and circumstances of obtaining the good intended

We now come to take notice of some wonderful circumstances of the attainment of our good hereby, which shows the great wisdom of the contrivance:

1. God has so contrived in this way that a sinful creature should become not guilty, and that he who has no righteousness of his own should become righteous. These things, if they had been proposed, would have appeared contradictious to any but the divine understanding.

If it had been proposed to any created intelligence to find out a way in which a sinful creature should not be a guilty creature, how impossible would it have been judged that there should be any way at all. It would doubtless have been judged impossible but that he who has committed sin must stand guilty of the sin he has committed. And if sin necessarily obliges to punishment, it must oblige him who has committed it. If punishment and sin are inseparable, then that punishment and the sinner are inseparable. If the law denounces death to the person who is guilty of sin, and if it is impossible that the law should not take place, then he who has committed sin must die. Thus any created understanding would have thought.

And if it had been proposed that there should be some way found out wherein man might be righteous without fulfilling righteousness himself, so that he might reasonably and properly be looked upon and accepted as a righteous person, and adjudged to the reward of righteousness, and yet have no righteousness, and yet have broken the law, and done nothing else but break it—this doubtless would have been looked upon as impossible and contradictory.

Yet the wisdom of God has truly accomplished each of these things. He has accomplished that men, though sinners, should be without guilt, in that he has found out a way that the threatenings of the law should truly and properly be fulfilled, and punishment be executed on sin, and yet not on the sinner. The sufferings of Christ answer the demands of the law, with respect to the sins of those who believe in Him. Justice is truly satisfied thereby, and the law is fulfilled and answered by the obedience of Christ, so that His righteousness should properly be our righteousness. Though not performed by us, yet it is properly and reasonably accepted for us, as much as if we had performed it ourselves. Divine wisdom has so contrived that such an interchanging of sin and righteousness should be consistent, and most agreeable with reason, with the law, and God's holy attributes. For Jesus Christ has so united Himself to us, and us to Him, as to make Himself ours, our Head. The love of Christ for the elect is so great that God the Father looks upon it proper and suitable to account Christ and the elect as one, and accordingly to account what Christ does and suffers as if they did it and suffered it. That love of Christ which is so great as to render Him willing to put Himself in the stead of the elect, and to bear the misery that they deserved, does, in the Father's account, so unite Christ and the elect that they may be looked upon as legally one.

2. It shows wonderful wisdom that our good should be procured by such seemingly unlikely and opposite means as the humiliation of the Son of God. When Christ was about to undertake that great work of redemption, He did not take the method that any creature wisdom would have thought as the most proper. Creature wisdom would have determined that, in order to His effectually and more gloriously accomplishing

such a great work, He should rather have been exalted higher, if it had been possible, rather than humbled so low. Earthly kings and princes, when they are about to engage in any great and difficult work, will put on their strength, and will appear in all their majesty and power that they may be successful. But when Christ was about to perform the great work of redeeming a lost world, the wisdom of God took an opposite method and determined that He should be humbled and abased to a mean state, and appear in low circumstances. He did not deck Himself with glory, but laid it aside. He emptied himself. Philippians 2:6–8: "Being in the form of God, He made Himself of no reputation, and took on Him the form of a servant, and was made in the likeness of men; and being found in fashion as a man, He humbled Himself and became obedient unto death, even the death of the cross." Creature wisdom would have thought that Christ, in order to perform this great work, should deck Himself with all His strength; but divine wisdom determined that He should be made weak, or put on the infirmities of human nature.

And why did divine wisdom determine that He should become thus weak? It was that He might be subject to want, to suffering, and to the power and malice of His enemies. But then what advantage could it be to Him in this work, to be subject to the power and malice of His enemies? It was the very design for which He came into the world, to overcome His enemies.

Who would have thought that this was the way to overthrow them, that He should become weak and feeble, and for that very end that He might be subject to their power and malice. But this is the very means by which God determined that Christ should prevail against His enemies, that He should be subject to their power, that they might prevail against Him so as to put him to disgrace, pain, and death.

What else but divine wisdom could ever have determined that this was the way to be successful in the work of our redemption. This would have appeared to creature wisdom as the most direct course to be frustrated that could be devised. But it was indeed the way to glorious success, and the only way. "The foolishness of God is wiser than men" (1 Corinthians 1:25). God has brought strength out of weakness, and glory out of ignominy and reproach. Christ's shame and reproach are the only means by which a way is made to our eternal honor.

The wisdom of God has made Christ's humiliation the means of our exaltation. His coming down from heaven is that which brings us to heaven. The wisdom of God has made life the fruit of death. The death of Christ was the only means by which we could have eternal life. The death of a person who was God was the only way by which we could come to have life in God. Here favor is made to rise out of wrath; our acceptance into God's favor out of God's wrath upon His own Son. A blessing rises out of curse; our everlasting blessedness, from Christ being made a curse for us. Our righteousness is made to rise out Christ's imputed guilt. He was made sin for us that we might be made the righteousness of God (2 Corinthians 5:21). By such wonderful means has the wisdom of God procured our salvation.

3. Our sin and misery by this contrivance are made an occasion of our greater blessedness. This is a very wonderful thing. It would have been a very wonderful thing if we had been merely restored from sin and misery, to be as we were before. But it was a much more wonderful thing that we should be brought to a higher blessedness than ever, and that our sin and misery should be the occasion of it, and should make way for it.

First, it was wonderful that sin should be made the occasion of our greater blessedness; for sin deserves misery. By our sin we had deserved to be everlastingly miserable. But this is so turned by divine wisdom that it is made an occasion of our being more happy. It was a strange thing that sin should be the occasion of anything else but misery. But divine wisdom has found out a way whereby the sinner might not only escape being miserable, but that he should be happier than before he sinned, yea than he would have been if he had never sinned at all. And this sin and unworthiness of his are the occasion of this greater blessedness.

Second, it was a wonderful thing that man's own misery should be an occasion of his greater happiness. For happiness and misery are contraries, and man's misery was very great. He was under the wrath and curse of God, and condemned to everlasting burning. But the sin and misery of man by this contrivance are made an occasion of his being more happy not only than he was before the fall, but than he would have been if he never had fallen.

Our first parents, if they had stood and persevered in perfect obedience till God had given them the fruit of the tree of life as a seal of their reward, would probably have been advanced to higher happiness. For they before were but in a state of probation for their reward. And it is not to be supposed but that their happiness was to have been greater after they had persisted in obedience, and had actually received the reward, than it was while they were in a state of trial for it. But by the redemption of Christ, the sin and misery of the elect are made an occasion of their being brought to a higher happiness than mankind would have had if they had persisted in obedience till they had received the reward, and that for these reasons:

- Man is hereby brought to a greater and nearer

union with God. If man had never fallen, God would
have remained man's friend. He would have enjoyed
God's favor, and so would have been the object of
Christ's favor, as he would have had the favor of all the
persons of the Trinity. But Christ has become our
Surety and Savior, and has taken on Him our nature,
which occasions between Christ and us a union of a
quite different kind, and a nearer relation than otherwise would have been. The fall is the occasion of
Christ's becoming our head and the church, His body.
And believers have become His brethren and spouse in
a manner that otherwise would not have been. And by
our union with Christ we have a greater union with the
natural Son of God. Galatians 4:4–6: "When the fullness
of time was come, God sent forth His Son, made of a
woman, made under the law, to redeem them that were
under the law, that we might receive the adoption of
sons. And because ye are sons, God hath sent forth the
Spirit of His Son into your hearts, crying, 'Abba,
Father.' " And therefore Christ has taught us, in all our
addresses to God, to call Him our Father in like manner as He calls Him Father. John 20:17: "Go tell My
brethren, behold, I ascend to My Father, and your
Father."

This is one of the wonderful things brought about
by the work of redemption, that thereby our separation
from God is made an occasion of a greater union than
was before, or otherwise would have been. When we fell,
there was dreadful separation made between God and
us; but this is made an occasion of a greater union.
John 17:20–23: "Neither pray I for these alone, but for
them also which shall believe on Me through their
word; that they all may be one, as Thou, Father, art in
Me, and I in Thee; that they also may be one in us, that
the world may believe that Thou hast sent Me. And the
glory which Thou gavest Me I have given them, that

they may be one, even as we are one. I in them, and
Thou in Me, that they may be made perfect in one."
   • Man now has greater manifestations of the glory
and love of God than otherwise he would have had. In
the manifestations of these two things, man's happiness principally consists. Now man, by the work of redemption, has greater manifestation of both than otherwise he would have had. We have already spoken particularly of the glory of God, and what advantages even
the angels have by the discoveries of it in this work. But
if they have such advantages, much more will man
have, who is far more directly concerned in this affair
than they are. Here are immediately greater displays of
the love of God than man had before he fell; or, as we
may well suppose, than he would have had if he had
never fallen. (God now manifests His love to His people
by sending His Son into the world to die for them.
There never would have been any such testimony of the
love of God if man had not fallen.)
   Christ manifests His love by coming into the world
and laying down His life. This is the greatest testimony
of divine love that can be conceived. Now surely the
greater discoveries God's people have of His love to
them, the more occasion will they have to rejoice in
that love. (Here will be a delightful theme for the saints
to contemplate to all eternity, which they never could
have had if man never had fallen: the dying love of
Christ. They will have occasion now to sing that song
forever found in Revelation 1:5–6: "Unto Him that loved
us, and washed us from our sins in His own blood, and
hath made us kings and priests unto God and His
Father, to whom be glory and dominion for ever.
Amen.")
   • Man now has greater motives offered him to love
God than otherwise he ever would have had. Man's
happiness consists in mutual love between God and

man, in seeing God's love to him and in reciprocally
loving God. And the more he sees of God's love to him,
and the more he loves God, the more happy must he be.
His love to God is as necessary to his happiness as seeing God's love for him. For he can have no joy in beholding God's love for him any otherwise than as he
loves God. This make the saints prize God's love for
them, for they love Him. If they did not love God, to see
His love for them would not make them happy. But the
more any person loves another, the more will he be delighted in the manifestations of that other's love.
There is provision therefore made for both in the work
of redemption. There are greater manifestations of the
love of God to us than there would have been if man
had not fallen. And also there are greater motives to
love Him than otherwise there would have been. There
are greater obligations to love Him for God has done
more for us to win our love. Christ has died for us.

Again, man is now brought to a more universal and
immediate and sensible dependence on God than otherwise he would have been. All his happiness is now of
Him, through Him, and in Him. If man had not fallen,
he would have had all his happiness of God by his own
righteousness. But now it is by the righteousness of
Christ. He would have had all his holiness of God, but
not so sensibly, because then he would have been holy
from the beginning, as soon as he received his being.
But now, he is first sinful and universally corrupt, and
afterwards is made holy. If man had held his integrity,
misery would have been a stranger to him. And therefore happiness would not have been so sensible a
derivation from God as it is now, when man looks to
God from the deeps of distress, cries repeatedly to Him,
and waits upon Him. He is convinced by abundant experience that he has no place of resort but God, who is
graciously pleased, in consequence of man's earnest

and persevering suit, to appear for his relief, to take him out of the miry clay and horrible pit, set him upon a rock, establish his goings, and put a new song into his mouth. By man's having thus a more immediate, universal, and sensible dependence, God more entirely secures man's undivided respect. There is now a greater motive for man to make God his all in all, to love Him and rejoice in Him as his only portion.

• By the contrivance for our salvation, man's sin and misery are but an occasion of his being brought to a more full and free converse with and enjoyment of God than otherwise would have been. For, as we have observed already, the union is greater; and the greater the union, the more full the communion and intimate the intercourse. Christ has come down to man in his own nature. And hereby he may converse with Christ more intimately than the infinite distance of the divine nature would allow. This advantage is more than what the angels have. For Christ is not only in a created nature, but He is in man's own nature. We have also advantages for a more full enjoyment of God. By Christ's incarnation, the saints may see God with their bodily eyes as well as by an intellectual view. The saints, after the day of judgment, will consist of both body and soul. They will have outward as well as spiritual sight. It is now ordered by divine wisdom that God Himself, or a divine person, should be the principal entertainment of both these kinds of sight, spiritual and corporal. And the saints in heaven shall not only have an intellectual sight of God, but they shall see a divine person as they see one another; not only spiritually, but outwardly. The body of Jesus Christ will appear with that transcendent visible majesty and beauty which is exceedingly expressive of the divine majesty, beauty, and glory. The body of Christ shall appear with the glory of God upon it, as Christ tells us in Matthew 16:27: "The

Son of man shall come in the glory of His Father."
Thus, to see God will be a great happiness to the saints.
Job comforted himself that he would see God with his
bodily eyes. Job 19:26: "And though after my skin,
worms destroy this body, yet in my flesh shall I see
God."

• Man's sin and misery are made an occasion of his
greater happiness, as he has now a greater relish of
happiness by reason of his knowledge of both. In order
to happiness, there must be two things, union to a
proper object and a relish of the object. Man's misery is
made an occasion of increasing both these by the work
of redemption. We have shown already that the union
is increased, and so is the relish too, by the knowledge
man now has of evil. These contraries, good and evil,
heighten the sense of one another. The forbidden tree
was called the tree of knowledge of good and evil. Of
evil, because by it we came to the experience of evil. Of
good, because we should never have known so well
what good was if it had not been for that tree. We are
taught the value of good by our knowledge of its contrary, evil. This teaches us to prize good, and makes us
the more to relish and rejoice in it. The saints know
something what a state of sin and alienation from God
is. They know something what the anger of God is, and
what it is to be in danger of hell. And this makes them
the more exceedingly to rejoice in the favor and in the
enjoyment of God.

Take two persons, one who never knew what evil
was, but was happy from the first moment of his being,
having the favor of God and numerous tokens of it; another who is in a very doleful and undone condition.
Let there be bestowed upon these two persons the same
blessings, the same good things. And let them be ob-
jectively in the same glorious circumstances; which will
rejoice most? Doubtless he who was brought to this

happiness out of a miserable and doleful state. So the
saints in heaven will forever the more rejoice in God,
and in the enjoyment of His love, for their being
brought to it out of a most lamentable state and condition.

SECTION 7
Some wonderful circumstances of the overthrow of Satan

The wisdom of God greatly and remarkably appears
in so exceedingly baffling and compounding all the
subtlety of the old serpent. Power never appears so conspicuous as when opposed and conquering opposition.
The same may be said of wisdom. It never appears so
brightly, and with such advantage, as when opposed by
the subtlety of some very crafty enemy, and in baffling
and confounding that subtlety. The devil is exceedingly
subtle. The subtlety of the serpent is emblematic of this
(Genesis 3:1). He was once one of the brightest intelligences of heaven, and one of the brightest, if not the
very brightest, of all. All the devils were once morning
stars, of a glorious brightness of understanding. They
still have the same faculties, though they ceased to be
influenced and guided by the Holy Spirit of God. And
so their heavenly wisdom is turned into hellish craft
and subtlety. God, in the work of redemption, has wondrously baffled the utmost craft of the devils, though
they all combined to frustrate God's designs of glory to
Himself and goodness to men. The wisdom of God appears very glorious herein for these reasons:
   1. Consider the weak and seemingly despicable
means and weapons that God employs to overthrow
Satan. Christ poured the greater contempt upon Satan
in the victory that He obtained over him by reason of

the means of His preparing Himself for it, and the
weapons He has used. Christ chooses to encounter
Satan in the human nature, in a poor, frail, afflicted
state. He did as David did. David, when going against
the Philistine, refused Saul's armor, a helmet of brass, a
coat of mail, and his sword. No, he put them all off.
Goliath came mightily armed against David, with a
helmet of brass upon his head, a coat of mail weighing
five thousand shekels of brass, greaves of brass upon
his legs, and a target of brass between his shoulders, a
spear, whose staff was like a weaver's beam, and the
spear's head weighing six hundred shekels of iron.
And besides all this, he had one bearing a shield before
him. But David took nothing but a staff in his hand,
and a shepherd's bag and a sling, and he went against
the Philistine.

So the weapons that Christ made use of were His
poverty, afflictions and reproaches, sufferings and
death. His principal weapon was His cross, the instrument of His own reproachful death. These were seemingly weak and despicable instruments to wield against
such a giant as Satan. And doubtless the devil disdained
them as much as Goliath did David's staves and sling.
But with such weapons as these Christ has, in a human,
weak, mortal nature overthrown and baffled all the
craft of hell.

Such disgrace and contempt has Christ poured
upon Satan. David had a more glorious victory over
Goliath, conquering him with such mean instruments;
and Samson over the Philistines, killing so many of
them with such a despicable weapon as the jaw-bone of
an ass. It is spoken of in Scripture as a glorious triumph
of Christ over the devil, that He should overcome him
by such a despicable weapon as His cross. Colossians
2:14–15: "Blotting out the handwriting of ordinances
that was against us, which was contrary to us, and took

it out of the way, nailing it to His cross: and having spoiled principalities and powers, He made a show of them openly, triumphing over them in it." God shows His great and infinite wisdom in taking this method to confound the wisdom and subtlety of His enemies. He hereby shows how easily He can do it, and that He is infinitely wiser than they. 1 Corinthians 1:27–28: "God hath chosen the foolish things of the world to confound the wise; and God hath chosen the weak things of the world to confound the things that are mighty: and the base things of the world, and things that are despised, hath God chosen; yea, and things that are not, to bring to nought the things that are."

2. (God has thereby confounded Satan with his own weapons.) It is so contrived in the work of redemption that our grand enemy should be made a means of his own confusion. By those very things whereby he endeavors to rob God of His glory and destroy mankind, he is made an instrument of frustrating his own designs. His most subtle and powerful endeavors for accomplishing his designs are made a means of confounding them and of promoting the contrary. Of this, I will mention but two instances.

First, (his procuring man's fall is made an occasion of the contrary to what he designed.) Indeed, he has hereby procured the ruin of multitudes of mankind, which he aimed at. But in this he does not frustrate God's design from all eternity to glorify Himself. And the misery of multitudes of mankind will prove no content to him, but will enhance his own misery.

What Satan did in tempting man to fall is made an occasion of the contrary to what he intended in that it gave occasion for God to glorify Himself all the more, and gives occasion for the elect being brought to higher happiness.

The happy state of man was envied by Satan. That

man, who was of earthly origin, should be advance to such honors when he who was originally of a so much more noble nature should be cast down to such disgrace, this his pride could not bear. How then would Satan triumph when he had brought man down!

The devil tempted our first parents with this, that if they would eat of the forbidden fruit they should be as gods. It was a lie in Satan's mouth. For he aimed at nothing else but to fool man out of his happiness, and make him his own slave and vassal, with a blinded expectation of being like a god. But little did Satan think that God would turn it so as to make man's fall an occasion of God's becoming man. And so an occasion of our nature was advanced to a state of closer union to God.

By this means it comes to pass that one in man's nature now sits at the right hand of God, invested with divine power and glory, and reigns over heaven and earth with God-like power and dominion. Thus is Satan disappointed in his subtlety. As he intended that saying, "Ye shall be as gods," it was lie to decoy and befool man. Little did he think that it would be in such manner verified by the incarnation of the Son of God. And this is the occasion also of all the elect being united to this divine person, so that they become one with Christ. Believers are as members and parts of Christ. Yea, the church is called Christ. Little did Satan think that his telling that lie to our first parents, "Ye shall be as gods," would be the occasion of their being members of Christ the Son of God.

Again, Satan is made a means of his own confusion in this. It was Satan's design in tempting man to sin to make man his captive and slave forever; to have plagued and triumphed over him. And this very thing is a means to bring it about, that man, instead of being his vassal, should be his judge. The elect, instead of being his captives, to be forever tormented and triumphed over by him, shall sit as judges to sentence him to everlasting torment. It has been the means that one in man's nature should be his supreme Judge. It was man's nature that Satan so envied, and sought to make a prey of. But Jesus Christ at the last day shall come in man's nature. And the devils shall be all brought to stand trembling at His bar. And He shall judge and condemn them, and execute the wrath of God upon them. And not only shall Christ in the human nature judge the devils, but all the saints shall judge them with Christ as assessors with Him in judgment. 1 Corinthians 6:3: "Know ye not that we shall judge angels?"

Second, in another instance Satan is made a means of his own confusion, that is, in his procuring the death of Christ. Satan set himself to oppose Christ as soon as He appeared. He sought by all means to procure His ruin. He set the Jews against Him. He filled the minds of the scribes and Pharisees with the most bitter persecuting malice against Christ. He sought by all means to procure His death, and that He might be put to the most ignominious death. We read "that Satan entered into Judas, and tempted him to betray Him" (Luke 22:3–4). And Christ speaks of His sufferings as being the effects of the power of darkness. Luke 22:53: "When I was daily with you in the temple, ye stretched forth no hands against Me; but this is your hour and the power of darkness." But Satan hereby overthrows his own kingdom. Christ came into the world to destroy the works of the devil. And the very thing that did it was the blood and death of Christ. The cross was the devil's own weapon. And with this weapon he was overthrown, just as David cut off Goliath's head with his own sword.

Christ thus making Satan a means of his own confusion was typified of old by Samson's getting honey

out of the carcass of the lion. There is more implied in
Samson's riddle, "Out of the eater came forth meat, and
out of the strong came forth sweetness," than ever the
Philistines explained. It was verified by Christ in a far
more glorious manner. God's enemies and ours are
taken in the pit which they themselves have dug. And
their own soul is taken in the net which they have laid.
Thus we have shown, in some measure, the wisdom of
this way of salvation by Jesus Christ.

SECTION 8
The superiority of this wisdom to that of the angels

The wisdom of this contrivance appears to have
been above the wisdom of the angels by the following
things:
1. It appears that the angels did not fully comprehend the contrivance till they saw it accomplished.
They knew that man was to be redeemed long before
Christ came into the world. But they did not fully comprehend it until they saw it. This is evident by the expression in the text: "That now might be known unto
the principalities the manifold wisdom of God." Now
the work is actually accomplished by Jesus Christ,
which implies that it was now new to them. If they understood no more of it now than they had all along, the
apostle would never have expressed himself so; for he is
speaking of it as a mystery, in a measure kept hidden
until now.
Considered that the angels had four thousand years
to contemplate this affair. And they did not lack inclination and desire to understand and look into it, as the
Scripture teaches us. They had also a great deal to put
them upon an attentive contemplation of it. For when
it was made known that God had such a design, it must

appear a new and wonderful thing to them. They had seen their fellow angels destroyed without mercy. And this redeeming of the fallen sinful creature was quite a new thing. It must have been astonishing to them when God had revealed this design of mercy to them presently after the fall. He had given an intimation of it in saying, "The seed of the woman shall bruise the serpent's head." They knew that God had such a design. For they were, from the beginning, ministering spirits, sent forth to minister to those who were the heirs of salvation. They were present at the institution of the typical dispensation that was so full of shadows of gospel truth (Psalm 69:17).

The angels contemplating the contrivance of our redemption was typified by the posture of the cherubim over the mercy seat, which was the lid of the ark. These emblems were made bending down towards the ark and mercy seat. This is what the Apostle Peter is thought to have some reference to in 1 Peter 1:12. Yet the angels, though for four thousand years they had been studying this contrivance, did not fully comprehend it till they saw it accomplished. This shows that the wisdom of it was far above theirs. For if they could not fully comprehend it after it had been revealed that there was such a design, and after much of it had already been made known in the Old Testament, how much less could they have found it out of themselves.

Consider for what end this wisdom of God was made known unto the angels, that they might admire and prize it. It was made known to them so that they might see how manifold, how great and glorious, it is; that they might see the unspeakable "depths of the riches of the wisdom and knowledge of God," as the apostle expresses it in Romans 11:33. It was manifested to them that they might see the glory of God in it, and how great and wonderful the mystery was. 1 Timothy 3:16:

"Great is the mystery of godliness: God was manifest in the flesh, justified in the spirit, seen of angels." Now if the wisdom of it was not far above their own understandings, this would not be shown them for the express purpose that they might admire and praise God for it.

2. It appears to be above the wisdom of the angels because they are still contemplating it, and endeavoring to see more and more of it. Indeed, there is room for their faculties to employ themselves to all eternity. It is evident from 1 Peter 1:11-2 that they are still employing themselves in endeavoring to see more and more of God's wisdom appearing in the work of redemption, "Searching what, or what manner of time the Spirit of Christ which was in them did signify, when it testified beforehand of the sufferings of Christ, and the glory that should follow. Unto whom it was revealed, that not unto themselves, but unto us they did minister the things, which are now reported unto you by them that have preached the gospel unto you, with the Holy Ghost sent down from heaven; which things the angels desire to look into." They still desire to look into it, after they have seen it accomplished. They do not so perfectly comprehend all the wisdom that is to be seen in it. But they are contemplating, looking into it, that they may see more and more. But there will still be room enough in this work to employ the angelical understandings.

SECTION 9
The subject improved

Hence we may learn the blindness of the world, that the wisdom appearing the work of redemption is no more admired in it. God has revealed His glorious design and contrivance to the world, sends forth His gospel, and causes it to be preached abroad in order to declare to the world that His infinite wisdom has been engaged for man's salvation. But how little is it regarded! There are some who have their eyes opened to behold the wondrous things of the gospel, who see the glory of God in it, and admire the wisdom of it. But the greater part are wholly blind to it. They see nothing in all this that is in any way glorious and wonderful. Though the angels account it worthy of their most engaged and deep contemplation, yet the greater part of men take little notice of it. It is all a dull story and dead letter to many of them. They cannot see anything in it above the wisdom of men. Yea, the gospel to many seems to be foolishness.

Though the light that shines in the world is so exceeding glorious, yet how few are there who see it. The glory of God's wisdom in this work is surpassing the brightness of the sun. But so blind is the world that it sees nothing. It does not know that the Son of righteousness shines. Thus it has been in all ages, and wherever the gospel has been preached, ministers of the Word of God in all ages have had occasion to say, "Who has believed our report, and to whom is the arm of the Lord revealed?" Thus the prophets were sent to many with that errand in Isaiah 6:9–10: "Go and tell this people, 'Hear ye indeed, but understand not; and see ye indeed, but perceive not.' Make the heart of this people fat, and their ears heavy, and shut their eyes; lest they should see with their eyes, and hear with their ears, and understand with their heart, and convert, and be healed."

When Christ that glorious prophet came, and more fully revealed the counsels of God concerning our redemption, how many were then blind! How much did Christ complain of them! How blind were the scribes and Pharisees, the most noted sect of men among the Jews for wisdom. They beheld no glory in that gospel which Christ preached unto them, which gave Him occasion to call them fools and blind in Matthew 23:17.

So it was again in the apostles' times. In all places where they preached, some believed and some did not (Acts 28:24). "As many as were ordained to eternal life believed" (Acts 13:48). "The election obtained, but the rest were blinded" (Romans 11:7). And so it is still in those places where the gospel is preached. There are a few who see the glory of the gospel. God has a small number whose eyes He opens, who are called out of darkness into marvelous light, and who have an understanding to see the wisdom and fitness of the way of life. But how many are there who sit under the preaching of the gospel all their days, yet never see any divine wisdom or glory in it! To their dying day they are unaffected with it. When they hear it, they see nothing to attract their attention, much less excite any admiration. To preach the gospel to them will serve very well to lull them to sleep, but produces very little other effect upon them. This shows the exceeding wickedness of the heart of man. How affecting the thought that infinite wisdom should be set on work so as to surprise the angels, and to entertain them from age to age, and that to men, though so plainly set before them, it should appear foolishness! 1 Corinthians 1:18: "The preaching of the cross is to them that perish foolishness."

This is a great confirmation of the truth of the gospel. The gospel stands in no need of external evidences of its truth and divinity. It carries its own light and evidence with it. There is that in its nature that sufficiently distinguishes it to those who are spiritually enlightened from all the effects of human invention. There are evident appearances of the divine perfections, the stamp of divine glory, of which this one of divine wisdom is not the least part.

There is as much in the gospel to show that it is no work of men as there is in the sun in the firmament. As persons of mature reason who look upon the sun, and consider the nature of it, its wonderful height, its course, its brightness and heat, may know that it is no work of man, so, if the gospel is duly considered, if the true nature of it is seen, it may be known that it is no work of man, and that it must be from God. And if the wisdom appearing in the gospel is duly considered, it will be seen as much to excel all human wisdom as the sun's light excels the light of fires of our own kindling. The contrivance of our salvation is of such a nature that no one can rationally conclude that man had any hand in it. The nature of the contrivance is such, so out of the way of all human thoughts, so different from all human inventions, so much more sublime, excellent, and worthy, that it does not savor at all of the craft or subtlety of man. It savors of God only.

If any are ready to think man might have found out such a way of salvation for sinners that was honorable to God, to His holiness and authority, they do not well consider the scantiness of human understanding. Mankind had no capacity for any such undertaking. For till the gospel enlightened the world, they had but miserable notions of what was honorable to God. They could have but poor notions of what way would be suitable to the divine perfections. For they were woefully in the dark about these divine perfections themselves till the gospel came abroad in the world. They had strange notions about a deity. Most of them thought there were many gods. "They changed the glory of the incorruptible God into an image like to corruptible man, and to birds and four-footed beasts and creeping things" (Romans 1:23). They attributed vices to God. Even the philosophers, their wisest men, entertained but imperfect notions of the Supreme Being. How then could men find out a way so glorious and honorable to God, and agreeable to His perfections, who did not have enough wisdom to get any tolerable notions of God till the gospel was revealed to them? They groped in the dark. Their notions showed the infinite insufficiency of man's blind understanding for any such undertaking as the contriving of a way of salvation every way honorable to God, and suitable to the needs of a fallen creature.

But since the gospel has told what God's counsels are, and how He has contrived a way for our salvation, men are ready to despise it, and foolishly to exalt their own understanding, and to imagine they could have found out as good a way themselves. Alas, men, of themselves, had no notion of what was honorable to God and suitable for a Divine Being! They did not so much as think of the necessity of God's law being answered and justice satisfied. And if they had, how dreadfully would they have been puzzled to have found out the way how! Who would have thought of a trinity of persons in the Godhead, and that one should sustain the rights of the Godhead, another should be the Mediator, and another should make application of redemption? Who would have thought of such a thing as three distinct persons and yet but one God, all the same Being, and yet three persons! Who would have thought of this as a way for satisfying justice? Who would have thought of a way for answering the law that threatened eternal death without the sinner's suffering eternal death? And who would have thought of any such thing as a divine person suffering the wrath of God? And if they had, who would have contrived a way how He should suffer, since the divine nature cannot suffer?

Who would have thought of any such thing as God becoming man, two natures and but one person? These things are exceedingly out of the way of human thought and contrivance. It is most unreasonable to think that the world who, till the gospel enlightened them, were so blind about the nature of God and divine things, should contrive such a way that should prove thus to answer all ends, every way to suit what the case required, most glorious to God, and answerable to all man's necessities. Everything is so fully provided for, and no absurdity to be found in the whole affair, but all speaking forth the most perfect wisdom. That there should be no infringement upon holiness or justice, nothing dishonorable to the majesty of God, no encouragement to sin, all possible motives to holiness, all manner of happiness provided, and Satan so confounded and entirely overthrown—how truly wonderful!

And if we suppose that all this notwithstanding was the invention of men, whose invention should it be? Who should be pitched upon as the most likely to invent it? It was not the invention of the Jews, for they were the most bitter enemies to it. The wise men among them, when they first heard of it, conceived malice against it till the apostles preached it to them. And it appeared a very foolish doctrine to the wise men among them. The doctrine of Christ crucified was not only to the Jews a stumbling block, but also to the Greeks foolishness (1 Corinthians 1:23). Besides, it was contrary to all their notions about a deity, and they knew nothing about the fall of man and the like till the gospel revealed it to them.

It was not the invention of the apostles, for the apostles, of themselves, were in no way capable of any such learned contrivance. They were poor fishermen and publicans, an obscure and illiterate sort of men, till they were extraordinarily taught. They were all surprised when they first heard of it. When they heard that

Christ must die for sinners, they were offended at it. And it was a long while before they were brought fully to receive it.

There is but one way left, and that is, to suppose that Christ was a mere man, a very subtle crafty man, and that He invented it all. But this is as unreasonable as the rest. For it would have been all against Himself to invent a way of salvation by His own crucifixion, a most tormenting and ignominious death.

Hence see how great a sin they are guilty of who despise and reject this way of salvation! When God has manifested such unsearchable riches of wisdom, when all the persons of the Trinity have held a consultation from all eternity in providing a way of salvation for us sinful, miserable worms; a way that should be sufficient and every way suitable for us; a way that should be in all things complete, whereby we might have not only full pardon of all our sins and deliverance from hell, but also full blessedness in heaven forever—how provoked God must be when, after all, men reject this way of salvation!

When salvation comes to be preached, and is offered to them in this way, when they are invited to accept its benefits and yet they despise and refuse it, they thus practically deny it to be a wise way, and call this wisdom of God foolishness—how provoking it must be when such a poor creature as man shall rise up and find fault with that wisdom which is so far above the wisdom of angels! This is one thing wherein consists the heinousness of the sin of unbelief, it implies rejecting and despising divine wisdom in the way of salvation by Jesus Christ. Unbelief finds fault with the wisdom of God in the choice of the person for performing this work. It dislikes the person of Christ. It sees no form nor comeliness in Him, nor beauty wherefore it should desire Him.

That person whom the wisdom of God looked upon
as the fittest person of any, the only fit person, is despised and rejected by unbelief. Men, through unbelief,
find fault with the salvation itself that Christ has purchased. They do not like to be saved as Christ would
save. They do not like to be made holy, and to have
such a happiness as is to be had in God for a portion.

It may not be amiss here to mention two or three
ways whereby persons are guilty of a provoking contempt of the wisdom of God in the way of salvation.

First, they are guilty of a provoking contempt who
live in a careless neglect of their salvation, who are secure in their sins, and are not much concerned about
either salvation or damnation. This is practically
charging God with folly. Its language is that all is in
vain, and it is to no purpose that God has contrived and
consulted for our salvation when there was no need of
it. They are well enough as they are. They do not see
any great necessity of a Savior. They like the state they
are in, and do not much desire to be delivered out of it.
They do not thank Him for all His consultation and
contrivance, and think He might have spared Himself
the cost. God has greatly minded that which they do
not think worth minding, and has contrived abundantly for that which they do not trouble their heads
about.

Second, they are guilty of provoking contempt of
the wisdom of this way of salvation who go about to
contrive ways of their own. They who are not content
with salvation by the righteousness of Christ, which
God has provided, are for contriving some way of being
saved by their own righteousness. These find fault with
the wisdom of God's way, and set up their own wisdom
in opposition to it. How greatly must God be provoked
by such conduct!

Third, those who entertain discouraged and despairing apprehension about their salvation cast contempt on the wisdom of God. They think that because they have been such great sinners, God will not be willing to pardon them and Christ will not be willing to accept of them. They fear that Christ, in the invitations of the gospel, does not mean such wicked creatures as they are; that because they have committed so much sin, they have sinned beyond the reach of mercy. They think it is in vain for them to seek for salvation, as though it were not all-sufficient; as though the wisdom of God had not found out a way that was sufficient for the salvation of great sinners.

SECTION 10
The misery of unbelievers

Unbelievers have no portion in this matter. There is a most glorious way of salvation, but you, who are unbelievers, have no interest in it. The wisdom of God has been gloriously employed for the deliverance of men from a miserable, doleful state. But you are never the better for it because you reject it. If you continue in that state, this wisdom will do you no good.

Christ is a glorious person, in every way fit to be a Savior of sinners, a person who has sufficient power, sufficient wisdom, sufficient merit, and sufficient love for perfecting this work. He is the only fit person, but you have no right in Him. You can lay claim to no benefit by His power, wisdom, love, or merits. This wisdom of God has found out a way whereby this Savior might satisfy justice and fulfill the law for us; but you have no lot in the incarnation, death, and sufferings of Jesus Christ.

The wisdom of God has contrived a way of salvation that there should be procured for us perfect and everlasting happiness. Here is a most glorious portion, the Divine Being Himself, with His glorious perfections. Here it is purchased that we should see God face to face, that we should converse and dwell with God in His own glorious habitation, that we should be the children of God and be conformed to Him. Here we have prepared all needed good for both the souls and bodies of sinners, all needed earthly good things while here, and glory for both body and soul hereafter forever.

But you are never the better for all this. You have no lot nor portion in any of it. Notwithstanding all this rich provision, you remain in the same miserable state and condition in which you came into the world. Though the provision of the gospel is so full, yet your poor soul remains in a famishing, perishing state. You remain dead in trespasses and sins, under the dominion of Satan, in a condemned state, having the wrath of God abiding on you, and being daily exposed to the dreadful effects of it in hell. Notwithstanding all this provision, you remain wretched and miserable, poor, blind and naked. Oh, that you might turn to God through Jesus Christ, be numbered among His disciples and faithful followers, and so be entitled to their privileges! They have an interest in this glorious Savior, and are entitled to all the ineffable blessedness of His kingdom, so far as their capacities will admit. But you remain without Christ, being aliens from the commonwealth of Israel, strangers to the covenant of promise, having no well-grounded hope, and without God in the world.

Further consider a few things:

• It argues the great misery of sinners that the wisdom of God should be exercised to such a degree in order to find out a way to deliver them from it. Their case surely was most deplorable, since it required infinite wisdom to find out a way for their deliverance. The wisdom of angels was not sufficient. Nothing but divine wisdom could reach and remedy their case. And all the persons of the Trinity entered into a consultation about it. If man's misery was not very great, divine wisdom would not have been exercised for his deliverance from it. God would not contrive and do things so wonderful in a trivial affair. If the salvation of a sinner were not a great salvation, from an exceedingly great misery, it is not to be supposed that God's wisdom should be more signalized in this affair than in any other whatever.

But so it is, this contrivance seems to be spoken of in Scripture as the masterpiece of divine wisdom. This work of redemption is represented as most wonderful, and spoken of in Scripture in the most exalted manner of any work of God. Doubtless, therefore, salvation is a great thing. And consequently the misery that sinners are saved from is a great and unspeakable misery. Now this is the misery that you are all in who remain in a natural condition. This is the condemnation you lie under. This is the wrath of God that abides upon you. The wisdom of God knew it to be a very doleful thing for a person to be in a natural state, and therefore did so exercise itself to deliver miserable sinners out of it. But this is the state that many among us do yet remain in.

• Consider that, if you continue in the state you are in, you will be so far from being the better for this contrivance, you will be much more miserable for it. The justice and wisdom of the way of salvation will be your condemnation. "This is the condemnation, that light is come into the world, and men loved darkness rather than light" (John 3:19). If you continue in the state that you are now in, it would have been better for you if Christ had never died for sinners, if God had left all mankind to perish, as He did the fallen angels. Your punishment then would have been light in comparison of what it will be now. You will have greater sins by far to answer for, and all your sins will be abundantly the more aggravated.

Since I have been upon this subject, I have observed that (the work of redemption is an occasion of the elect being brought to greater happiness than man could have had if he had not fallen) And it is also true as to reprobates, that it will be an occasion of their having greater misery that they would have had if there had been no redemption. 2 Corinthians 2:15: "For we are unto God a sweet savor of Christ in them that are saved, and in them that perish. To the one we are a savor of death unto death; and to the other we are a savor of life unto life." If you perish at last, you will be the more miserable for the benefits of the gospel being so glorious, and that because your crime in rejecting and despising them will be the more heinous. Hebrews 2:3: "How shall we escape, if we neglect so great salvation."

• While you continue as an unbeliever, the more you hear of this way of salvation, your condition will become the more miserable. The longer you sit under the preaching of the gospel, the more doleful your case grows. Your guilt continually increases, for your refusal of the gospel and your rejections of this way of salvation are so much the oftener repeated. Every time you hear the gospel preached, you are guilty of renewed rejection of it, the guilt of which therefore you will have lying upon you. And the more you hear of the suitableness and glory of this way, the greater is your guilt who still continue to reject it. Every new illustration of the wisdom and grace of God in redemption adds to your guilt. Matthew 23:37: "O Jerusalem, Jerusalem, how often would I have gathered thy children together, even as a hen gathereth her chickens under her wings, but ye would not!" What adds to your misery is that, as long as it continues, it is a growing evil.

• Consider the danger there is, that you will never have any lot or portion in this matter, seeing there are but few who have. Christ has told us that strait is the gate and narrow is the way that leads unto life, and "few there be that find it." There have been but few in all ages of the world. Many seek, and many hope that they shall obtain. There are but few who intend to be damned, while many hope that they shall some way or other find means to escape eternal misery. But after all, there are but few saved, or who obtain the benefits of redemption.

SECTION 11
Exhortation to come to Christ

I conclude with a use of exhortation to come to Christ, and accept salvation in this way. You are invited to come to Christ, heartily to close with Him, and trust in Him for salvation. And if you do so, (you shall have the benefit of all, as much as if the whole had been contrived for you alone.) God has already contrived everything that is needful for your salvation. And there is nothing wanting but your consent. Since God has taken this matter of the redemption of sinners into His own hands, He has made thorough work of it. He has not left it for you to finish. Satisfaction is already made, righteousness is already wrought out, death and hell are already conquered. The Redeemer has already taken possession of glory, and keeps it in His hands to bestow on them who come to Him. There were many difficulties in the way, but they are all removed. The Savior has already triumphed over all, and is at the right hand of God, to give eternal life to His people.

Salvation is already brought to your door, and the

Savior stands, knocks, and calls that you would open to Him, so that He might bring it in to you. There remains nothing but your consent. All the difficulty now remaining is with your own heart. If you perish now, it must be wholly at your door. It must be because you would not come to Christ that you might have life, and because you virtually choose death rather than life. Proverbs 8:36: "He that sinneth against me wrongeth his own soul: all they that hate me love death." All that is now required of you is that your heart should close with Christ as a Savior.

Consider that the wisdom of God has so contrived that He has forestalled all your objections. If you make objections against Christ and the way of salvation, they must all be unreasonable. You cannot reasonably object that your sins are of such a nature that God's honor will not allow for your pardon. It is true, God insists upon His own honor. He is a God who will be honored, and His majesty shall be vindicated. And when sinners cast contempt upon Him, His honor may be repaired by the punishment of sin without the sinner's suffering, however great the sin is. Herein the wisdom of this way appears, that there is a sufficiency for the greatest and most heinous transgressors.

You cannot object that God the Father will not be willing to accept you for the Mediator's sake, for He has chosen His own Son to be a mediator, to cut off any such objections. So you may be sure that God will receive you if you go to Him through Christ. You cannot object that God the Father has not given sufficient assurance of salvation to believers. For the principal things, those which would have been most difficult to believe, are already fulfilled. God has already given His Son to die for us. This, before it was accomplished, was much more strange and difficult to believe than that He should give eternal life to sinners after Christ died for them. Romans 8:32: "He that spared not His own Son, but delivered Him up for us all, how shall He not with Him freely give us all things."

There is no room to doubt but that if we accept Christ God will give eternal life. For He has given it already into the hands of our Savior for us. He has entrusted Him with the whole affair. He has given all things into His hands so that He might give eternal life to as many as should come to Him. The Father has appointed Him who died for believers to be their Judge, to have the whole determination of the matter, and the disposal of the reward, in His own hand. And you cannot doubt but that Christ will be willing to bestow eternal life on them for whom He purchased it. For if He is not willing to bestow it, surely He never would have died to purchase it. Who can think that Christ would be so desirous of sinners being saved as to undergo so much for it, and not be willing to let them have it when He had obtained it for them.

Consider that the wisdom of God has contrived that there should be in the person of the Savior all manner of attractives to draw us to Him. He has in Him all possible excellency. He is possessed of all the beauty and glory of the Godhead, so that there can be no manner of excellency, nor degree of excellency that we can devise, but what is in the person of the Savior. Yet so redundant has the wisdom of God been in providing attractives, in order that we should come to Christ, it has so ordered that there should also be all human excellencies in Him. If there is anything attractive in the consideration that Christ is one in our own nature, one of us, this is true of Christ. He is not only in the divine nature, but in the human nature. He is truly a man, and has all possible human excellencies. He was of a most excellent spirit, wise and holy, condescending and meek, and a lowly, benign, and benevolent disposition.

The wisdom of God has chosen a person of great love to sinners, and who would show that love in the most endearing manner possible. What more condescending love can there be than the love of a divine person to such worms in the dust? What greater love can there be than dying love? And what more endearing expression of love can there be than dying for the beloved? The wisdom of God has so contrived that Christ shall sustain that office which should most tend to endear Him to us, and draw us to Him: the office of a redeemer from eternal misery, and the purchaser of all happiness.

And if all this is not enough to draw us, the wisdom of God has ordered more. It has provided us a Savior who should offer Himself to us in the most endearing relation. He offers to receive us as friends, to receive us to a union to Himself, to become our spiritual husband and portion forever. And the wisdom of God has provided us a Savior who woos in a manner that has the greatest tendency to win our hearts. His word is most attractive. He stands at our door and knocks. He does not merely command us to receive Him, but He condescends to apply Himself to us in a more endearing manner. He entreats and beseeches us in His Word and by His messengers.

The wisdom of God has contrived that there should be all manner of attractives in the benefits that Christ offers you. There are not only the excellencies of the person of Christ to draw you to Him, but the desirable benefits He offers. Here is what is most suitable to the cravings of the human nature. Men, when distressed and burdened, long for ease and rest. Here it is offered to us in Christ: "Come unto Me", says He, "all ye that labor and are heavy laden, and I will give your rest." Men, when in fear of danger, long for safety. Here it is provided for us in Christ. God promises that He will become a shield and buckler, a strong rock and high tower to those who trust in Him. Those who mourn need comfort. Christ tells us that He came to comfort those who mourn (Isaiah 61:2). The blind need to have their eyes opened. The light is sweet to men. Christ offers to anoint our eyes with eye salve so that we may see glorious light. He will be our sun, and the light of God's countenance. What is more dear to men than life? Christ has purchased for men that they should live forever. Psalm 21:4: "He asked life of thee and thou gavest it him, even length of days for ever and ever." How greatly is a crown prized and admired by the children of men! And Christ does not offer a corruptible crown, but an incorruptible and far more glorious crown than any worn by earthly kings; a crown of glory, the luster of which shall never fade nor decay; with an everlasting kingdom. Do men love pleasures? Here are pleasures forevermore. What could there be more to draw our hearts to Jesus Christ, and to make us willing to accept Him for our Savior, with all His unspeakable benefits?

The Justice of God
In Making Satisfaction for Sin

Justice requires that sin be punished, because sin deserves punishment. What the demerit of sin calls for, justice calls for, for it is only the same thing in different words. The notion of deserving punishment is the very same as a just connection with punishment. None will deny but that there is such a thing, in some cases, as the desert or demerit of a crime, its calling for or requiring punishment. And to say that the desert of a crime requires punishment is just the same thing as to say the reason why it requires it is that it deserves it. So that the suitableness of the connection between the crime and the punishment consists in the desert, and therefore, wherever desert is, there is such suitableness.

None will deny that some crimes are so horrid, and so deserving of punishment, that it is requisite that they should not go unpunished, unless something very considerable be done to make up for the crime—either some answerable repentance, or some other compensation, that in some measure at least balances the desert of punishment, and so, as it were, takes it off or disannuls it. Otherwise the desert of punishment remaining, all will allow that it is fit and becoming, and to be desired, that the crime should be severely punished. And why is it so, but only from the demerit of the crime, or because the crime so much deserves such a punishment? It justly excites so great abhorrence and indignation that it is requisite there should be a punishment answerable to this abhorrence and indignation that is fitly excited by it. But by this, all is granted that needs to be granted to show that desert of punishment carries in

166

it a requisiteness of the punishment deserved. For if greater crimes very much require punishment because of their great demerit, lesser crimes will also require punishment, but only in a lesser degree, proportionate to their demerit, because the ground of the requisiteness of the punishment of great crimes is their demerit. It is requisite that they should be punished on no other account but because they deserve it.

And besides, if it is allowed that it is requisite that great crimes should be punished with punishment in some measure answerable to the heinousness of the crime, without something to balance them (some answerable repentance or other satisfaction), because of their great demerit and the great abhorrence and indignation they justly excite, it will follow that it is requisite that God should punish all sin with infinite punishment because all sin, as it is against God, is infinitely hateful to Him, and so stirs up infinite abhorrence and indignation in Him. Therefore, it is requisite that God should punish it unless there is something in some measure to balance this desert: either some answerable repentance and sorrow for it, or other compensation. Now there can be no repentance of it, or sorrow for it, in any measure answerable or proportionable to the heinousness of the demerit of the crime because that is infinite, and there can be no infinite sorrow for sin in finite creatures. Yea, there can be none but what is infinitely short of it, none that bears any proportion to it. Repentance is as nothing in comparison to it, and therefore can weigh nothing when put in the scales with it, and so does nothing at all towards compensating it or diminishing the desert or requisiteness of punishment, any more than if there were no repentance. If any asks why God could not pardon the injury on repentance without other satisfaction, without any wrong to justice, then I ask the same person, why He could not also pardon the injury without repentance? For the same reason, could He not pardon with repentance without satisfaction? (For all the repentance men are capable of is no repentance at all, or is as little as none, in comparison to the greatness of the injury, for it bears no proportion to it. And it would be as dishonorable and unfit for God to pardon the injury without any repentance at all, as to do it merely on the account of a repentance that bears no more proportion to the injury than none at all.) Therefore, we are not forgiven on the grounds of our repentance because it in any wise compensates, takes off, or diminishes the desert or requisiteness of punishment, but because of the respect that evangelical repentance has to compensation already made.

If sin, therefore, deserves punishment, that is the same as to say that it is fitting and proper that it should be punished. If the case is so that sin deserves punishment from men, in those cases it is proper it should receive punishment from men. A fault cannot be properly said to deserve punishment from any but those to whom it belongs to inflict punishment when it is deserved. In those cases, therefore, wherein it belongs to men to inflict punishment, it is proper for them to inflict that punishment that is deserved of them.

Again, if sin's desert of punishment is the proper ground of the fitness of its connection with punishment, or rather is that wherein fitness of the connection consists, it will thence follow not only that it is fitting that sin that deserves punishment should be punished, but also that it should be punished as it deserves.

It is fitting that a person's state should be agreeable to the quality of his dispositions and voluntary actions. Suffering is suitable and answerable to the quality of sinful dispositions and actions. It is suitable that they who will evil and do evil should receive evil in proportion to the evil that they will or do. It is but justice that it should be so and, when sin is punished, it receives but its own, or that which is suitably connected with it. But it is a contradiction to say that it is suitably connected with punishment, or that it is suitable that it should be connected with it, and yet that it is suitable it should not be connected with it. All sin may be resolved into hatred of God and our neighbor, as all our duty may be resolved into love to God and our neighbor. And it is but fitting that this spirit of enmity should receive a return in its own kind, that it should receive enmity again. Sin is of such a nature that it wishes ill, and aims at all to God and man, but to God especially. It strikes at God. It would, if it could, procure His misery and death. It is but suitable that with what measure it metes, it should be measured to it again. It is but suitable that men should reap what they sow, and that the rewards of every man's hand should be given to him. This is what the consciences of all men naturally declare. There is nothing that men know sooner, after they come to the exercise of their reason, than that, when they have done wickedness, they deserve punishment. The consciences not only of Christians, and those who have been educated in the principles of divine revelation, but also the consciences of heathens, inform them of this. Therefore, unless conscience has been stupified by frequent violations when men have done wickedness, there remains a sense of guilt upon their minds, a sense of an obligation to punishment. It is natural to expect that which conscience or reason tells them it is suitable should come, and therefore they are afraid and jealous, and ready to flee when no man pursues.

Seeing, therefore, it is requisite that sin should be punished, as punishment is deserved and just, therefore the justice of God obliges him to punish sin. For it belongs to God, as the Supreme Ruler of the universality of things, to maintain order and decorum in His kingdom, and to see to it that decency and righteousness take place in all cases. That perfection of His nature, whereby He is disposed to this, is His justice; therefore His justice naturally disposes Him to punish sin as it deserves.

The holiness of God, which is the infinite opposition of His nature to sin, naturally and necessarily disposes Him to punish sin. Indeed, His justice is part of His holiness. But when we speak of God's justice inclining Him to punish sin, we have respect only to that exercise of His holiness whereby He loves that holy and beautiful order that consists in the connection of one thing with another according to their nature, and so between sin and punishment, and His opposition to that which would be so unsuitable as a disconnection of these things. But now I speak of the holiness of God as appearing not directly and immediately in His hatred of an unsuitable, hateful disconnection between sin and that which is proper for it, but in His hatred of sin itself, or the opposition of His nature to the odious nature of sin.

If God's nature is infinitely opposite to sin, then doubtless He has a disposition answerable to oppose it in His acts and works. If He by His nature is an enemy to sin with an infinite enmity, then He is doubtless disposed to act as an enemy to it, or to do the part of an enemy to it. And if He is disposed naturally to do the part of an enemy against sin, or, which is the same thing, against the faultiness or blameworthiness of moral agents, then it will follow that He is naturally disposed to act as an enemy to those who are the persons faulty and blameworthy, or are chargeable with the guilt of it, as being the persons faulty. Indignation is the proper exercise of hatred of anything as a fault or thing blamable, and there could be no such thing either in the Creator or creature as hatred of a fault without indignation, unless it is conceived or hoped that the fault is suffered for, and so the indignation is satisfied. Whoever finds a hatred to a fault, and at the same time imputed the fault to him who committed it, therein feels an indignation against him for it. So that God, by His necessary, infinite hatred of sin, is necessarily disposed to punish it with a punishment answerable to His hatred.

It does not become the Sovereign of the world, a Being of infinite glory, purity, and beauty, to suffer such a thing as sin, an infinitely uncomely disorder, an infinitely detestable pollution, to appear in the world subject to His government, without His making an opposition to it, or giving some public manifestations and tokens of His infinite abhorrence of it. If He should so do, it would be countenancing it, which God cannot do, for "He is of purer eyes than to behold evil, and cannot look on iniquity" (Habakkuk 1:13). It is natural in such a case to expect tokens of the utmost opposition. If we could behold the infinite Fountain of purity and holiness, and could see what an infinitely pure flame it is, and with what a pure brightness it shines, so that the heavens appear impure when compared with it, and then should behold some infinitely odious and detestable filthiness brought and set in its presence, would it not be natural to expect some ineffably vehement opposition to it? And would not the lack of it be indecent and shocking?

If it is to God's glory that He is in His nature infinitely holy and opposite to sin, then it is to His glory to be infinitely displeased with sin. And if it is to God's glory to be infinitely displeased with sin, then it must be to His glory to exercise and manifest that displeasure and to act accordingly. But the proper exercise and testimony of displeasure against sin in the Supreme Being and absolute Governor of the world is taking vengeance. Men may show their hatred of sin by lamenting it, mourning for it, and taking great pains and undergoing great difficulties to prevent or remove it, or by approving God's vengeance for it. Taking vengeance is not the proper way of fellow subjects' hatred of sin, but it is in the Supreme Lord and Judge of the world, to whom vengeance belongs, because He has the ordering and government of all things; and therefore, suffering sin to go unpunished would in Him be a conniving at it. Taking vengeance is as much the proper manifestation of God's displeasure at sin as a mighty work is the proper manifestation of His power or as a wise work is the proper manifestation of His wisdom. There may be other testimonies of God's displeasure with the abhorrence of sin without testifying His displeasure in condign punishment. He might declare that He has such a displeasure and abhorrence. So there might be other testimonies of God's power and wisdom besides a powerful wise effect. He might have declared Himself to be infinitely wise and powerful. But yet there would have been lacking the proper manifestations of God's power and wisdom if God had only declared Himself to be possessed of these attributes. The creatures might have believed Him to be all-wise and almighty, but by seeing His mighty and wise works, they see His power and wisdom. So if there had been only a declaration of God's abhorrence and displeasure against sin, the creature might have believed it, but could not have seen it unless He should also take vengeance for it.

The honor of the greatness, excellency, and majesty of God's being requires that sin be punished with an infinite punishment. If we consider sin as leveled against God, not only compensative justice to the sinner, but justice to Himself requires that God should punish sin with infinite punishment. Sin casts contempt on the majesty and greatness of God. The language of it is that He is a despicable being, not worthy to be honored or feared, not so great that His displeasure is worthy to be dreaded, and that His threatenings of wrath are despicable. Now the proper vindication or defense of God's majesty in such a case is for God to contradict this language of sin in His providence towards sin that speaks this language, or to contradict the language of sin in the event and fruit of sin.

Sin says that God is a despicable being, and not worthy that the sinner should fear Him, and so affronts Him without fear. The proper vindication of God's majesty then is for God to show that He is worthy that the sinner should regard Him and fear Him by appearing in a fearful, dreadful event to the person who is guilty to show that He is an infinitely fearful and terrible being. The language of sin is that God's displeasure is not worthy that the sinner should regard it. The proper vindication of God from this is to show, by the experience of the event, the infinite dreadfulness of that slighted displeasure. In such a case, the majesty of God requires this vindication. It cannot be properly vindicated without it; neither can God be just to Himself without this vindication, unless there could be such a thing as a repentance, humiliation, and sorrow for this proportionate to the greatness of the majesty despised. When the majesty of God has such contempt cast upon it, and is trodden down in the dust by vile sinners, it is not fitting that this infinite and glorious Majesty should be left under this contempt, but that it should be vindicated wholly from it, and that it should be raised perfectly from the dust wherein it is trodden by something opposite to the contempt which is equivalent to it, or of weight sufficient to balance it—

either an equivalent punishment, or an equivalent sorrow and repentance. So sin must be punished with an infinite punishment.

Sin casts contempt on the infinite glory and excellency of God. The language of it is that God is not an excellent being, but an odious one, and therefore, that it is no heinous thing to hate Him. Now it is fitting that on this occasion omniscience should declare and manifest that it judges otherwise, and that it should show that it esteems God as infinitely excellent, and therefore, that it looks on it as an infinitely heinous thing to cast such a reflection on God by infinite tokens of resentment of such a reflection and such hatred.

God is to be considered in this affair not merely as the Governor of a world of creatures, to order things between one creature and another, but as the Supreme Regulator and Rector of the universe, the orderer of things relating to the whole compass of existence, including Himself. He is to maintain the rights of the whole, and decorum through the whole, and to maintain His own rights and the due honor of His own perfections as well as to preserve justice among His creatures. It is fitting that there should be one who has this office, and this office properly belongs to the Supreme Being. And if He should fail to do justice to Himself in a necessary vindication of His own majesty and glory, it would be an immensely greater failure of His rectoral justice than if He should deprive the creatures (that are beings of infinitely less consequence) of their right.

There is a necessity of sin's being punished with a condign punishment from the law of God that threatens such punishment. All but Epicureans will own that all creatures who are moral agents are subjects of God's moral government, and that therefore He has given a law to His creatures, and that law must have sanctions;

it must be enforced with threatenings of punishment. Otherwise it fails of having the nature of a law and is only of the nature of counsel or advice, or rather of a request. For one being to express his inclination or will to another, concerning anything he would receive from him, any love or respect, without any threatening annexed, but leaving it with the person as to whether he will afford it or not, whether he will grant it or not, supposing that his refusal will be with impunity, is properly of the nature of a request. It does not amount to counsel or advice because when we give counsel to others, it is for their interest. But when we express our desire or will of something we would receive from them, with impunity to them whether they grant it or not, this is more properly requesting than counseling. No doubt it falls far short of the nature of lawgiving. For such an expression of one's will as this is an expression of will without any expression of authority. It holds forth no authority for us merely to manifest our wills or inclinations to another, nor indeed does it exhibit any authority over a person to promise him rewards. So persons may, and often do, promise rewards to others for doing those things that they have no power to oblige them to. So may persons do to their equals, and so may a king do to others who are not his subjects. This is bargaining with others rather than giving them laws.

That expression of will only is a law which is exhibited in such a manner as to express the lawgiver's power over the person to whom it is manifested, expressing his power of disposal according as the other person complies or refuses; that which shows power over him, so as to oblige him to comply, or to make it be to his cost if he refuses.

For the same reason that it is necessary that the divine law should have a threatening of condign punishment annexed, it is also necessary that the threatening should be fulfilled. For the threatening wholly relates to the execution. If it had no connection with execution, it would be wholly void, and would be as no threatening; and so far as there is not a connection with execution, whether that be in a greater or lesser degree, so far and in such a degree it is void, and so far approaches the nature of no threatening as much as if that degree of unconnection was expressed in the threatening. For instance, if sin fails of threatened punishment half the times, this makes void the threatening in one half of it, and brings it down to be no more than if the threatening had expressed only so much that sin should be punished half the times that it is committed.

But if it is needful that all sin in every act should be forbidden by law, with a prohibition and threatening of condign punishment annexed, and that the threatening of sin with condign punishment should be universal, then it is necessary that it should be universally executed. A threatening of an omniscient and true being can be supposed to signify no more punishment than is intended to be executed, and is not necessarily to be understood of any more. A threatening, if it signifies anything, is a signification of some connection between the crime and the punishment. But the threatening of an omniscient being cannot be understood to signify any more connection with punishment than there is.

If it be needful that there should be a divine law, it is needful that this divine law should be maintained in the nature, life, authority, and strength that is proper to it as a law. The nature, life, authority, and strength of every law consists in its sanction, by which the deed is connected with the compensation, and therefore depends on the strength and firmness of the connection.

In proportion as that connection is weak, in such proportion the law loses its strength, fails of the proper nature and power of a law, and degenerates towards the nature of requests and expressions of will and desire to receive love and respect, without being enforced with authority.

Dispensing with the law by the lawgiver, so as not to fulfill it or execute it, in its nature does not differ from an abrogation of it, unless the law contains in itself such a clause that it shall or may be dispensed with and not fulfilled in certain cases, or when the lawgiver pleases. But this would be a contradiction. For if the law contained such a clause, then not to fulfill it would be according to the law and fulfillment of the law, and therefore there would be no dispensing with the law in it, because it is doing what the law itself directs to. The law may contain clauses of exception, wherein particular cases may be excepted from general rules, but it cannot make provision for a dispensation. And therefore, for the lawgiver to dispense with it is indeed to abrogate it. Though it may not be an abrogating of it wholly, yet it is in some measure changing it. To dispense with the law in not fulfilling it on him who breaks it is making the rule give place to the sinner. But certainly it is an indecent thing that sin, which provokes the execution, should procure the abrogation of the law.

It is necessary that the law of God should be maintained and executed, and not dispensed with or abrogated for the sake of the sinner, for the following reasons:

First, the nature and being of the law requires it. For as has been already shown, by such dispensation it loses the life and authority of a law, as it respects the subject. But it not only fails of being a law in this respect, it fails of being a rule to the Supreme Judge. The law is the great rule of righteousness and decorum that the Supreme and Universal Rector has established and published for the regulation of things in the commonwealth of the universality of intelligent beings and moral agents, in all that relates to them as concerned one with another. It is a rule by which things are not only to be regulated between one subject and another, but between the king and subjects, so that it may be a rule of judgment to the one as well as a rule of duty to the other. It is but reasonable to suppose that such a rule should be established and published for the benefit of all who belong to this universal commonwealth, to be a rule to direct both their actions towards each other and their expectations from each other, so that they may have a fixed and known rule by which they are to act and to be dealt with, to be both active and passive as members of this commonwealth. The subject is most nearly concerned not only in the measure of his own actions, but also in the consequences of them, or the method of his judge's determinations concerning him.

None who own the existence of a divine law, with threatenings annexed, can deny that there actually is such a rule as this that relates to both the manner of the creature's acting and the judge's acting toward him as subject to that law. For none will deny that the precepts relate to the manner of the subject's acting, and that the threatenings relate to the manner of the judge's proceeding with the subject in consequence of his obedience or disobedience.

It is needful that this great rule for managing affairs in this universal commonwealth should be fixed and settled, and not vague and uncertain. So far as it fails of this, it ceases to be of the nature of a rule. For it is essential to the nature of a rule that it be something fixed. But if it is needful that it is something fixed, then it is needful that the author, and he by whom it subsists, should maintain and fulfill it, and not depart from it, because that is in a measure to disannul it. If he does so, therein the rule becomes unfixed, and it so far ceases to be a rule to the judge.

Second, that the law should be made to give place to the sinner is contrary to the direct design of the law. For the law was made that the subject should be regulated by it and give place to it, and not to be regulated by the subject and to give place to him, especially to a wicked, vile, rebellious subject.

The law is made so that it might prevent sin and cause it not to be, and not that sin should disannul the law and cause it not to be. Therefore it would be very indecent for the Supreme Rector to cause this great rule to give place to the rebellion of the sinner.

Third, it is in no way fitting that this great rule should be abrogated and give place to the opposition and violation of the rebellious subject on account of the perfection of the lawgiver. The holiness of rectitude and goodness of this great rule, which the Supreme Lawgiver has established for the regulation of the commonwealth of moral agents, and its universal fitness, wisdom, and absolute perfection, render a partial abrogation for the sake of them who dislike it and will not submit to it needless and unseemly. If the great rule should be set aside for the sake of the rebel, it would carry too much of the face of acknowledgment in the lawgiver, of want of wisdom and foresight, or of some defect in point of holiness or righteousness in his law. He who breaks the law finds fault with it and casts the reflection on it that it is not a good law; and if God should in part abrogate the law upon this account, it would have too much of the appearance of a conceding to the sinner's objection against it. But God will magnify His law and make it honorable, and will give no occasion for any such reflections upon it, nor leave the law under such a reflection.

If this great rule of righteousness is so excellent and good a law, it is not only unfit that it should give place to rebellion, since this would be a dishonor to the excellency of the law and lawgiver, but also a wrong to the public good, which the Supreme Rector of the world has the care of and is the guardian of. If the rule is perfect, perfectly right and just and holy, and with infinite wisdom adapted to the good of the whole, then the public good requires that it be strongly established. The more firmly it is settled, and the more strongly it is guarded and defended, the better, and the more is it for the public good. And everything by which it is weakened is a damage and loss to the commonwealth of beings.

But I have already shown how every departure from it weakens it, unfixes it, and causes it to fail of the nature of a settled rule, and in some measure disannuls it.

Fourth, the sacredness of the authority and majesty of the Divine Lawgiver requires that He should maintain and fulfill His law when it is violated by a rebellious subject. I have spoken of the greatness and majesty of His being, and how that is concerned in it. I now would consider the sacredness of His authority, as He stands related to His creatures as their Lawgiver. The majesty of a ruler consists very much in that which appears in him that tends to strike the subject with reverence and awe, and dread of contempt of him or rebellion against him. And it is fitting that this awe and dread should be in proportion to the greatness and dignity of the ruler, and the degree of authority with which he is vested. But this awe and dread is by an apprehension of the terrible consequences, or the degree of the danger of those terrible consequences, or the degree of connection of that rebellion with those consequences. Therefore, if it is fitting that this awe or this apprehension should be in proportion to the greatness and dignity of the ruler, then it is fitting that the consequences of contempt of the Supreme Ruler of the world should be infinitely terrible, and the danger that it brings of punishment, or connection that it has with it, is strong and certain, and consequently, that the threatenings which enforce his laws should be sure and inviolable.

It is fitting the authority of a ruler should be sacred proportionally to the greatness of that authority, that is, in proportion to the greatness of the ruler, his worthiness of honor and obedience, the height of his exaltation above us, the absoluteness of his dominion over us, and the strength of his right to our submission and obedience. But the sacredness of the authority of a sovereign consists in the strength of the enforcement if it, and guard that is about it, that is, in the consequences of the violation to him who is guilty, and the degree of danger of these consequences. For the authority of a ruler does not consist in the power or influence he has on another by attractives, but coercives. The fence that is about the authority of a prince, that guards it as sacred, is the connection there is between the violations of it and the terrible consequences, or, in other words, in the strength of sureness of the threatening. Therefore, if this connection is partly broken, the fence is partly broken; in proportion as the threatenings are weak, the guard is weak.

But certainly it is fitting that the authority of the infinitely great and absolute Lord of heaven and earth should be infinitely sacred, and a fence without any breach in it. And it is not becoming the sacredness of the majesty and authority of the great Lawgiver that that perfectly holy, just, and infinitely wise and good law which He has established as the great rule for the regulation of all things in the universal commonwealth of beings should be set aside, to give place to the infinitely unreasonable and vile opposition that sinners make to it, and their horrid and daring rebellion against it.

Fifth, the truth of the lawgiver makes it necessary that the threatening of the law should be fulfilled in every punctilio. The threatening of the law is absolute: "Thou shalt surely die." It is true that the obligation does not lie in the claim of the person threatened as it is in promises, for it is not to be supposed that the person threatened will claim the punishment threatened. And indeed, if we look upon things strictly, those seem to reckon the wrong way who suppose the necessity of the futurity of the execution to arise from an obligation on God to execute properly consequent on His threatening. For the necessity of the connection of the execution with the threatening seems to arise directly the other way, from the obligation that was on the omniscient God in threatening consequent on the futurity of the execution. Though, strictly speaking, He is not obliged to execute because He has threatened, yet He was obliged not absolutely to threaten if He, at the same time, knew that He should not and would not execute, because this would not have been consistent with His truth.

So that from the truth of God, there is an inviolable connection between absolute threatening and execution, not so properly from an obligation on God to conform the execution to the past absolute threatening as from His obligation to conform His absolute threatening to the future execution. This God was absolutely obliged to do, as He would speak the truth. For if God absolutely threatened contrary to what He knew would come to pass, then He absolutely threatened contrary to what He knew to be true. And how any can speak contrary to what they know to be the truth in declaring, promising, or threatening, or in any other way consistently with perfect and inviolable truth I cannot conceive. Threatenings are significations of something, and if they are made consistent with truth, or are true significations of anything, they are significations of truth, or significations of that which is true. If absolute threatenings are significations of anything, they are significations of the futurity of the thing threatened. But if the futurity of the thing threatened is not true, then how can the threatenings be true significations? And if God in them speaks contrary to what He knows, and contrary to what He intends, then how He can speak true is to me inconceivable.

It is with absolute threatenings as it is with predictions. When God has foretold something that shall come to pass hereafter which does not concern our interest, and so is of the nature neither of a promise nor threatening, there is a necessary connection between the prediction and the fulfillment, but not by virtue of any claim we have to make, and so not properly by virtue of any obligation to fulfill consequent on the prediction, but by virtue of any obligation on an omniscient Being in predicting consequent on what He knew He would fulfill, an obligation to conform the prediction to the future event. It is as much against the veracity of God absolutely to threaten what He knows He will not accomplish as to predict what He knows He will not accomplish; for to do either would be to declare that that will be which He at the same time does not intend shall be. Absolute threatenings are a sort of prediction. God in them foretells or declares what shall come to pass. In a threat, the end of foretelling is to deter us from sinning. Absolute threatenings are God's declarations of something future, and the truth of God as much obliges Him to keep the truth in declarations of what is future as of what is past or present. For things

past, present, and future are all alike in God's view. And
when God declares to others what He sees Himself, He
is equally obliged to truth, whether the thing declared
is past, present, or to come. And, indeed, there is no
need of the distinction between present truth and
future in this case. For if any of God's absolute
threatenings are not to be fulfilled, those threatenings
are declarations or revelations contrary not only to
future truth, but such a threatening is a revelation of
the futurition of a punishment. That futurition is now
present with God. And if He signifies that a thing is
future which He knows is not future, then the
signification He gives is contrary to present truth, even
contrary to what God now knows is future. Again, an
absolute threatening is a signification of the present
intention of him who threatens; and therefore, if he
threatens what he does not intend to fulfill, then he
signifies an intention to be which is not, and so the
threatening is contrary to the present truth. God's absolute threatenings are a revelation to His subjects of
the appointed measures of their Judge's proceeding
with respect to their breaches of His law. And if they do
not reveal what is indeed the intended method of the
Judge's proceeding, then it is not a true revelation.

There is a necessity of the fulfillment of God's absolute promises both ways: both by an obligation on God
to foretell or declare (or foredeclare) the future benefit,
according to what He foresaw would be and He intended should be, and also by an obligation on Him to
fulfill His promise consequent on His predicting, and
by virtue of the claim of the person to whom the
promise was made.

There is also an obligation on God to fulfill His absolute threatenings consequent on His threatenings
indirectly, by virtue of many ill and undesirable consequences of the event's being, beside the certain depen-

dence or certain expectations raised by God's threatenings in the persons threatened, and others who are spectators, which consequences God may be obliged not to be a cause of. But threatenings do not properly bring an obligation on God that is consequent on them as threatenings as it is with promises.

As to those threatenings that are not positive or absolute, they are not necessarily followed with the punishment mentioned in them because the possibility of escaping the punishment is either expressed or understood in the threatening. But divine truth makes it necessary that there should be a certain connection between them, that as much punishment be inflicted as is signified by them. If certain suffering is not signified by them, then there is no necessary connection between them and certain suffering. If it is only signified in them that there is great danger of the suffering according to God's ordinary method of dealing with men, and that therefore they, as they would act rationally, have great reason to fear it, seeing that God does not see cause to reveal what He will do to them; if this is all that is really contained and understood in the threatening, then this is all that the threatening is connected with. Or if the proper meaning of the threatening is that such suffering shall come unless they repent, and this is all that can be fairly understood, then the truth of God makes nothing more necessary. But God's truth makes a necessary connection between every threatening and every promise, and all that is properly signified in that threatening or promise.

Christ makes full atonement

That Christ indeed suffered the full punishment of the sin that was imputed to Him, or offered that to God that was fully and completely equivalent to what we owed to divine justice for our sins, is evident by Psalm 69:5: "Oh God, Thou knowest my foolishness, and my sins [my guiltiness, it is in the Hebrew] are not hid from Thee." That the person who is the subject of this psalm, and who is here speaking is the Messiah, is evident from many places in the New Testament, in which it is applied to Christ. See John 15:25; John 2:17; Romans 15:3; 2 Corinthians 6:2; John 19:28–30 with Matthew 27:34, 48; Mark 15:23; Romans 11:9–10; Acts 1:20. And by the psalm itself, especially when compared with other psalms and prophecies of the Old Testament, it is plain that David, in this psalm, did not speak in his own name, but in the name of the Messiah.

But if it is the Messiah who is here speaking, then by the sin and guiltiness that He here speaks of must be intended not sin that He Himself committed, but that sin that was laid upon Him, or that He took upon Him, spoken of in Isaiah 53. And when Christ says, "Oh, God, Thou knowest my foolishness, and my guiltiness is not hid from Thee," it must mean that God did not forgive that which was imputed to Him, but punished it. When God forgives sin and does not execute punishment for it, then He is said not to behold iniquity nor see perverseness, to cover, hide, and bury their sins so that they cannot be seen or found, to turn away His face from beholding them, and not to remember them any more. But when God does not remit sin, but punishes it, then, in the language of the Old Testament, He is said to find out their sins, to set them before Him in the light of His countenance, to remember them, to bring them to remembrance, and to know them. And therefore, when it is said here, "Oh, God, Thou hast known my foolishness, and my guiltiness hast Thou not hid," thereby is intended that He forgives nothing

to the Messiah, but beholds all His guiltiness by imputed sin, has set all in the light of His countenance,
and does not cover or hide the least part of it.

God declares that those sinners who are not forgiven shall pay the uttermost farthing and the last mite,
and that all the debt shall be exacted of them. Now it
seems unreasonable to suppose that God, in case of a
surety and of His insisting on an atonement made by
Him, will show mercy by releasing the surety without a
full atonement, any more than than He will show
mercy to the sinner who is punished by not insisting
on the complete punishment.

A real atonement or satisfaction to God's justice was
necessary, and God did not design that, in His manner
of dealing with mankind, men should be pardoned and
accepted without atonement. God abundantly testified
by the sacrifices from the beginning of the world that
an atonement for sin was necessary, and must be insisted on in order to His acceptance of the sinner. This
proves that a sacrifice of infinite value was necessary,
and that God would accept no other. For an atonement
that bears no proportion to the offense is no atonement. An atonement carries in it a payment or satisfaction in the very notion of it. And if satisfaction was so
little necessary that the Divine Majesty easily admitted
one who bears no proportion at all to the offense, who
was wholly equivalent to nothing when compared with
the offense, and so was no payment or satisfaction at
all, then He might have forgiven sin without any
atonement. And then an atonement could not be so
greatly to be insisted upon, as is represented by all the
prodigious expense and labor, the multitude of services
and ceremonies, so great an apparatus, and so great
pomp, which with so much exactness were prescribed
to be continued through so many ages, respecting their
typical sacrifices and atonements, and from God's

church were propagated through the world of mankind.

That no mere creature could offer to God that true sacrifice of real atonement of which the Old Testament sacrifices were resemblances or shadows is evident by the Old Testament. For by the Old Testament it is evident that that is not sufficient to be looked upon by God as any real atonement or sacrifice for sin which is God's before it is offered to Him. In Psalm 50 we have a prophecy of Christ's coming to set up His kingdom in the world. There it is said in the fifth verse and following: "Gather My saints together unto Me: those that have made a covenant with Me by sacrifice" (where we may observe that the necessity of sacrifices is implied). "And the heavens shall declare His righteousness; for God is judge Himself. Selah. 'Hear, O My people, and I will speak; O Israel, and I will testify against thee. I am God, even thy God. I will not reprove thee for thy sacrifices, or thy burnt offerings, to have been continually before Me. I will take no bullock out of thy house, nor he goats out of thy folds. For every beast of the forest is Mine, and the cattle upon a thousand hills. I know all the fowls of the mountains, and the wild beasts of the field are Mine. If I were hungry, I would not tell thee; for the world is Mine, and the fulness thereof.' " But no mere creature can have anything to offer to God which is not His already, for all that he has is God's gift to him.

It is represented in Scripture that we are washed from our filthiness in Christ's blood. Whereas, although the blood of Christ washes from our guilt, yet it is the Spirit of Christ that washes from the pollution and stain of sin. However, the blood of Christ washes also from the filth of sin, since it purchases sanctification. It makes way for it by satisfying, and purchases it by the merit of obedience implied in it. The sacrifices under the law typified Christ's sacrifice not only as a satisfaction, but as meritorious obedience. They are called a sweet savor upon both these accounts. And therefore we find obedience compared with sacrifice in Psalm 40:6.

The sacrifice of Christ is a sweet savor because, as such, it was a great honor done to God's majesty, holiness, and law, and a glorious expression of Christ's respect to that majesty. Christ loved man and so greatly desired his salvation, and Christ had so great a respect to that majesty and holiness of God, that He would rather die than that the salvation of man should be any injury or dishonor unto those attributes. It was a sweet savor also since it was a marvelous act of obedience, and some expression of a wonderful respect to God's authority. The value of Christ's sacrifice was infinite, both as a propitiation and as an act of obedience, because He showed an infinite regard to the majesty and holiness of God, in being willing to pay out an infinite expense out of regard to those divine attributes.

It was needful that Christ be a Mediator between two parties that are distant and alienated one from the other, to be the middle person to unite them together, so that He Himself could be united to both. Otherwise He could not, by coming between them, be a bond of union between them. And if He is a Mediator between God and guilty men, it was necessary that He should unite Himself to them, or assume them as it were to Himself. But if He unites Himself to guilty creatures, He of necessity brings their guilt on Himself. If He unites Himself to them who are in debt, He brings their debt on Himself. He cannot properly unite Himself to a rebel against God, and one who is inclined to God's wrath, and is condemned to condign punishment, to be a Mediator to bring God to be at peace with him, without voluntarily taking his sufferings on Himself; because otherwise, His undertaking for such a one, and uniting Himself to such a one, will appear like countenancing his offense and rebellion. But if at the same time that He unites Himself to the sinner He takes it upon Himself to bear the sinner's penalty, it quite takes off all such appearance. He shows that though He loves the rebel who has affronted the Divine Majesty, yet He at the same time has the greatest possible abhorrence of the injury to God's majesty, and dishonor to His name, in that He regards the honor of God's majesty so much as to be willing to endure so extreme sufferings that the divine glory and majesty may not be injured, but fully maintained.

How Christ bore the wrath of God

Christ suffered the wrath of God for men's sins in such a way as He was capable of, being an infinitely holy person who knew that God was not angry with Him personally. He knew that God did not hate Him, but infinitely loved Him. The wicked in hell will suffer the wrath of God, as they will have the sense, knowledge, and sight of God's infinite displeasure toward them and hatred of them. But this was impossible in Jesus Christ. Christ therefore could bear the wrath of God in no other but in these two ways:

1. He had a great and clear sight of the infinite wrath of God against the sin of men, and the punishment they deserved. It was most fitting that He should have this at the time when He was suffering their stead, and paying their ransom to deliver them from that wrath and punishment; that He might know what He did, that He might act with full understanding at the time when He made expiation and paid a ransom for sinners to redeem them from hell.

It was requisite that at that time He should have a

clear sight of the dreadful evil and odiousness of that sin that He suffered for; that He might know how much it deserved the punishment; that it might be real and actual grace in Him; and that he undertook and suffered such things for those who were so unworthy and so hateful, which it could not be if He did not know how unworthy they were. It was also requisite that He should have a clear sight of the dreadfulness of the punishment that He suffered to deliver them from; otherwise He would not know how great a benefit He gave them in redeeming them from this punishment, and so it could not be actual grace in Him to bestow so great a benefit upon them since He would not have known how much He bestowed, and would have acted blindfold in giving so much. Therefore Christ, doubtless, actually had a clear view of both those things in the time of His last suffering; everything in the circumstances of His last suffering concurred to give Him a great and full sight of the evil and hateful nature of the sin of man. For its odious and malignant nature never appeared so much in its own proper colors as it did in that act of murdering the Son of God, and in exercising such contempt and cruelty towards Him.

Likewise, everything in the circumstances of His last sufferings tended to give Him a striking view of the dreadful punishment of sin. The sight of the evil of sin tended to this, and so did the enduring of temporal death, which is a great image of eternal death, especially under such circumstances with such extreme pain: God's hiding His face, His dying a death that by God's appointment was an accursed death, having a sight of the malice and triumph of devils, and being forsaken by His friends. As God ordered external circumstances to help forward this purpose, so there is all reason to think that His own influences on Christ's mind were agreeable hereto, His spirit acting with His

providence to give Him a full view of these things. Now
the clear view of each of these must of necessity be in-
expressibly terrible to the man Christ Jesus. His having
so clear an actual view of sin and its hatefulness was an
idea infinitely disagreeable to the holy nature of Christ,
and therefore, unless balanced with an equal sight of
good that comes by this evil, must have been an immensely disagreeable sensation in Christ's soul, or,
which is the same thing: immense suffering. But that
equally clear idea of good to counterbalance the evil of
sin was not given at that time, because God forsook
Christ and hid Himself from Him, and withheld com-
fortable influences or the clear ideas of pleasant objects. Thus did Christ bear our sins. God laid on Him
the iniquities of us all, and He bore the burden of
them. So His bearing the burden of our sins may be
considered as something diverse from His suffering
God's wrath; for His suffering wrath consisted more in
the sense He had of the other thing, that is, the dreadfulness of the punishment of sin, or the dreadfulness of
God's wrath inflicted for it. Thus Christ was tormented
not only in the fire of God's wrath, but in the fire of our
sins, and our sins were His tormentors. The evil and
malignant nature of sin was what Christ endured immediately, as well as more remotely, in bearing its consequences.

Thus Christ suffered that which the damned in hell
do not suffer. For they do not see the hateful nature of
sin. They have no idea of sin in itself, that is infinitely
disagreeable to their nature, as the idea of sin was to
Christ's holy nature, though conscience in them is
awakened to behold the dreadful guilt and desert of
sin. And as the clear view of sin in its hatefulness necessarily brought great suffering on the holy soul of
Christ, so also did the view of its punishment. For both
the evil of sin and the evil of punishment are infinite

evils, and both are infinitely disagreeable to Christ's nature—the former to His holy nature, or His nature as God, the latter to His human nature, or His nature as man. Such is human nature that a great, clear, and full idea of suffering, without some other pleasant and sweet idea to balance it, brings suffering, as appears from the nature of all spiritual ideas. They are repetitions (in a degree at least) of the things themselves of which they are ideas. Therefore, if Christ had a perfectly clear and full idea of what the damned suffer in hell, the suffering He would have had in the mere presence of that idea would have been perfectly equal to the thing itself, that is, if there had been no idea in Christ in any degree to balance it such as some knowledge of the love of God, of a future reward, future salvation of His elect, or so on. But pleasant ideas being in a great measure withheld by reason of God's hiding his face, hence the awful ideas of the eternal death which His elect people deserved, and of the dismal wrath of God, of consequence filled the soul of Christ with an inexpressible gloom.

Though Christ knew the love of God for Him, and knew He would be successful in His sufferings, yet when God forsook Him, those dismal views, those gloomy ideas, so fixed and swallowed up His mind that, though He had the habitual knowledge of those other objects, yet He could not attend to them. He could have comparatively but little comfort and support from them, for they could afford support no farther than they were attended to or were in actual view.

Christ's great love and pity for the elect (that His offering Himself up on the cross was the greatest act and fruit of, and consequently which He was then in the highest exercise of) was one source of His suffering. A strong exercise of love excites a lively idea of the object beloved. And a strong exercise of pity excites a lively idea of the misery under which he pities them. Christ's love then brought His elect infinitely near to Him in that great act and suffering wherein He especially stood for them and was substituted in their stead. And His love and pity fixed the idea of them in His mind as if He had really been they, and fixed their calamity in His mind as though it really was His. A very strong and lively love and pity towards the miserable tends to make their case ours as in other respects, so in this in particular, since it does in our idea place us in their stead, under their misery, with a most lively feeling sense of that misery, as it were feeling it for them and actually suffering it in their stead by strong sympathy.

Hence we may see how the same thing, the same ideas that distressed the soul of Christ and brought on His amazing sufferings, engaged Him to go through them. It was ordered that the bitterness of the cup, though exceedingly dreadful, was of that nature, or consisted in that; tasting that bitterness was the thing that engaged Him to go on to drink up the cup, and that as the bitterness of it arose from each of the aforementioned things. It arose from the clear idea He had then given to Him of the infinitely hateful and dreadful nature of sin. The more lively this idea was, the more dreadful it was to the soul of Christ. And yet, the more lively His idea of the hatefulness and dreadfulness of sin was, which consisted in disobedience to God, the more it engaged Him not to disobey Himself that great command He had received of His Father, that He should drink this cup and go through those sufferings.

The more He had a sense of how dreadful it is to condemn the authority of God and to dishonor His holy name, the more He would be engaged to remove and abolish this dishonor, and to honor the authority of God Himself. The more He had a sense of what an

odious and dreadful thing sin was, the more His heart
would be engaged to do and suffer what was necessary
to take away this dreadful and odious thing from those
His heart was united to in love, those whom the Father
had given Him. It was the lively exercise of love and pity
to those whom the Father had given Him that partially
occasioned so lively a view of the punishment they had
exposed themselves to, whereby His soul was filled with
a dismal sense, and so He suffered. But this lively love
and pity at the same time engaged Him to suffer for
them so as to deliver them from their deserved punishment that He had an idea of. And as pity towards His
elect excited a lively idea of their misery, so, on the
other hand, the increase of this idea of their misery excited strong exercises of pity, and this pity engaged
Him still to endure those sufferings in their stead.

From what has been said, we may learn how Christ
was sanctified in His last sufferings. The suffering of
His soul in great part consisted in the great and dreadful sense and idea that He then had given Him of the
dreadful, horrid odiousness of sin, which was done by
the Spirit of God. But this could not be without a proportionate increase of His aversion to and hatred of
sin, and consequently of His inclination to the contrary, which is the same thing as an increase of the holiness of His nature. Beside the immediate sight He
had given Him of the odious nature of sin, He had that
strong sense and that great experience of the bitter
fruit and consequences of sin to confirm His enmity to
it. Moreover He was then in the exercise of His highest
act of obedience or holiness, which, tending to increase the principle, the bringing forth of such great
and abundant fruit, tended to strengthen and increase
the root. Those last sufferings of Christ were in some
respects like a fire to refine the gold. For though the
furnace purged away no dross or filthiness, yet it in-

creased the preciousness of the gold; it added to the finite holiness of the human nature of Christ. Hence
Christ calls His offering Himself up His "sanctifying
Himself." John 17:19: "And for their sakes I sanctify
Myself, that they also may be sanctified through the
truth." Hence He calls those last sufferings a baptism
that He was to be baptized with. It was a baptism to Him
in two respects, as it purged Him from imputed guilt,
and as it increased His holiness by the Spirit of God,
who gave Him those terrible but sanctifying views. And
so this is one way in which the Captain of our salvation
is made perfect by sufferings (Hebrews 2:10 and 5:9;
Luke 13:32). Thus Christ, before He was glorified, was
prepared for that high degree of glory and joy He was to
be exalted to by first being sanctified in the furnace.

2. Another way in which it was possible that Christ
should endure the wrath of God was to endure the effects of that wrath. All that He suffered was by the special ordering of God. There was a very visible hand of
God in letting men and devils loose upon Him at such
a rate, and in separating Him from His own disciples.
Thus it pleased the Father to bruise Him and put Him
to grief. God dealt with Him as if He had been exceedingly angry with Him, and as though He had been the
object of His dreadful wrath. This made all the sufferings of Christ the more terrible to Him, because they
were from the hand of His Father whom He infinitely
loved, and whose infinite love He had had eternal experience of. Besides, it was an effect of God's wrath that
He forsook Christ. This caused Christ to cry out once
and again, "My God, My God, why hast Thou forsaken
Me?" This was infinitely terrible to Christ. Christ's
knowledge of the glory of the Father, His love for the
Father, and the sense and experience He had had of
the worth of the Father's love for Him, made the with-
holding of the pleasant ideas and manifestations of His

Father's love as terrible to Him as the sense and knowledge of His hatred is to the damned, who have no knowledge of God's excellency, no love for Him, nor any experience of the infinite sweetness of His love.

It was a special fruit of the wrath of God against our sins that He let loose the devil upon Christ, who has the power of death, who is God's executioner, and the roaring lion that devours the damned in hell. Christ was given up to the devil as his captive for a season. This antitype of Jonah was thrown to this great leviathan to be swallowed up as his prey. The time of Christ's suffering was the time of the prevalency of the power of the devil wherein Christ was delivered up to that power, as implied in Luke 22:53: "When I was daily with you in the temple, ye stretched no hands against Me; but this is your hour, and the power of darkness." And therefore, when Christ's last sufferings were approaching, Christ said in John 14:30, "The prince of this world cometh." He was let loose to torment the soul of Christ with gloomy and dismal ideas. He probably did his utmost to contribute to raise His ideas of the torments of hell.

(The most proper and clear trial of the measure of love or regard for the interest of another is the measure of suffering, or expense of personal interest, for the interest of the beloved.) So much as the lover regards the welfare of the beloved, so much in value or weight of his own welfare will he be willing to part with for it. If the value of the welfare obtained be, in regard to the sufferer, fully equal to the value of the welfare parted with, then, there being an equal balance, no preponderation of self-love will hinder parting with one for the other. The love therefore is sufficient and equal to self-love.

Heaven Is God's House

"In My Father's house are many mansions." John 14:2

In these words may be observed two things:

The thing described: Christ's Father's house. Christ spoke to His disciples in the foregoing chapter as one who was about to leave them. He told them in verse 31, "Now is the Son of Man glorified, and God is glorified in Him," and then gave them counsel to live in unity and love one another. By this they seemed somewhat surprised and hardly knew what to make of it. One of them, Peter, asked Him where He was going. Verse 36, "Simon Peter said unto Him, 'Lord, whither goest Thou?' " Christ did not directly answer and tell him where He was going, but He signified where in the verse 12. He told them plainly that He was going to His Father.

We may observe the description given of it: in it there are many mansions. The disciples seemed very sorrowful at the news of Christ's going away, but Christ comforted them by telling them that in His Father's house where He was going there was not only room for Him, but room for them too. There were many mansions. There was not only a mansion there for Him, but there were mansions enough for them all; there was room enough in heaven for them. When the disciples perceived that Christ was going away, they manifested a great desire to go with Him, particularly Peter. Peter, in the latter part of the foregoing chapter, asked Him where He was going, to that end that he might follow Him. Christ told Him that where He went Peter could not follow Him now, but that he should follow Him afterwards. But Peter, not content with that, seemed to have a great mind to follow Him now. "Lord," said he, "why cannot I follow Thee now?" So the disciples had a great mind still to be with Christ, and Christ in the words of the text intimates that they shall be with Him. Christ signified to them that He was going home to His Father's house, and He encouraged them that they shall be with Him there in due time, in that there were many mansions there. There was a mansion provided not only for Him, but for them all (for Judas was not then present), and not only for them, but for all who would ever believe in Him to the end of the world. Though He went before them, He only went to prepare a place for them who would follow.

The text is a plain sentence; 'tis therefore needless to press any doctrine in other words from it. So I shall build my discourse on the words of the text. There are two propositions contained in the words: (1) Heaven is God's house; and (2) in God's house there are many mansions.

1. Heaven is God's house. A house of public worship is a house where God's people meet from time to time to attend on God's ordinances; it is set apart for that and is called God's house. The temple of Solomon was called God's house. God was represented as dwelling there. There He has His throne in the holy of holies, even the mercy seat over the ark and between the cherubims.

Sometimes the whole universe is represented in Scripture as God's house, built with various stories one above another. Amos 9:6: "It is He that buildeth His stories in the heaven." Psalm 104:3: "Who layeth the beams of His chambers in the waters." But the highest heaven is especially represented in Scripture as the house of God. As to other parts of the creation, God has appointed them to inferior uses; but this part He has reserved for Himself for His own abode. We are told that the heavens are the Lord's, but the earth He has given to the sons of men. God, though He is everywhere present, is represented both in Old Testament and New as being in heaven in a special and peculiar manner. Heaven is the temple of God. Thus we read of God's temple in heaven in Revelation 15:5. Solomon's temple was a type of heaven. The Apostle Paul, is his epistle to the Hebrews, from time to time calls heaven "the holy of holies," as being the antitype not only of the temple of Solomon, but of the most holy place in that temple which was the place of God's most immediate residence. Hebrews 9:12: "He entered in once into the holy place." Verse 24: "For Christ is not entered into the holy places made with hands, which are the figures of the true, but into heaven itself."

Houses where assemblies of Christians worship God are in some respects figures of this house of God above. When God is worshipped by them in spirit and truth, they become the outworks of heaven and, as it were, its gates. As in houses of public worship here there are assemblies of Christians meeting to worship God, so in heaven there is a glorious assembly, or church, continually worshipping God: Hebrews 12:22–23: "But ye are come unto mount Sion, the city of the living God, the heavenly Jerusalem, and to an innumerable company of angels, to the general assembly and church of the first-born, that are written in heaven."

Heaven is represented in Scripture as God's dwelling-house. Psalm 113:5: "Who is like unto the Lord our God, who dwelleth on high." Psalm 123:1: "Unto Thee I lift up mine eyes, O Thou that dwellest in the heavens." Heaven is God's palace. 'Tis the house of the great King of the universe; there He has his throne, which is therefore represented as His house or temple. Psalm 11:4: "The Lord is in His holy temple; the Lord's throne is in heaven."

Heaven is the house where God dwells with His family. God is represented in Scripture as having a family; and though some of this family are now on earth, yet in so being they are abroad and not at home, but are all going home.) Ephesians 3:15: "Of whom the whole family in heaven and earth is named." Heaven is the place that God has built for Himself and His children. God has many children, and the place designed for them is heaven; therefore the saints, being the children of God, are said to be of the household of God. Ephesians 2:19: "Now therefore ye are no more strangers and foreigners, but fellow-citizens with the saints, and of the household of God." God is represented as a householder or head of a family, and heaven is His house.

Heaven is the house not only where God has His throne, but also where He keeps His table, where His children sit down with Him at His table, and where they are feasted in a royal manner becoming the children of so great a King. Luke 22:30: "That ye may eat and drink at My table in My kingdom." Matthew 26:29: "But I say unto you, I will not drink henceforth of this fruit of the vine until that day when I drink it new with you in My Father's kingdom."

God is the King of kings, and heaven is the place where He keeps his court. There are His angels and archangels that, as the nobles of His court, attend upon Him.

2. There are many mansions in the house of God. By many mansions is meant many seats or places of abode. As it is a king's palace, there are many mansions. Kings' houses are wont to be built very large, with many stately rooms and apartments. So there are many mansions in God's house.

When this is spoken of heaven, it is chiefly to be understood in a figurative sense, and the following things seem to be taught us in it:

(1) There is room in God's house for great numbers. There is room in heaven for a vast multitude, yea, room enough for all mankind that are or ever shall be. Luke 14:22: "Lord, it is done as Thou hast commanded, and yet there is room."

It is not with the heavenly temple as it often is with houses of public worship in this world, that they fill up and become too small and scanty for those who would meet in them, so that there is not convenient room for all. There is room enough in our heavenly Father's house. This is partly what Christ intended in the words of the text, as is evident from the occasion of His speaking them. The disciples manifested a great desire to be where Christ was, and Christ therefore, to encourage them that it should be as they desired, told them that in His Father's house where He was going were many mansions, that is, room enough for them.

There is mercy enough in God to admit an innumerable multitude into heaven. There is mercy enough for all, and there is merit enough in Christ to purchase heavenly happiness for millions of millions, for all men who ever were, are, or shall be. There is a sufficiency in the Fountain of heaven's happiness to supply and fill and satisfy all; and there is in all respects enough for the happiness of all.

(2) There are sufficient and suitable accommodations for all the different sorts of persons who are in the world: for great and small, high and low, rich and poor, wise and unwise, bond and free, persons of all nations, all conditions, and circumstances; for those who have been great sinners as well as for moral persons; for weak saints and those who are babes in Christ, as well as for those that are stronger and more grown in grace. There is in heaven a sufficiency for the happiness of every sort; there is a convenient accommodation for every creature that will hearken to the calls of

the gospel. None who will come to Christ, let His condition be what it will, needs to fear but that Christ will provide a place suitable for him in heaven. This seems to be another thing implied in Christ's words. The disciples were persons of very different conditions from Christ. He was their Master, and they were His disciples. He was their Lord, and they were the servants. He was their Guide, and they were the followers. He was their Captain, and they were the soldiers. He was the Shepherd, and they were the sheep. He was the Father, and they were the children. He was the glorious, holy Son of God, and they were the poor, sinful, corrupt men. Yet, though they were in such different circumstances from Him, Christ encouraged them that there shall not only be room in heaven for Him, but for them too; for there were many mansions there. There was not only a mansion to accommodate the Lord, but the disciples also; not only the Head, but the members; not only the Son of God, but those who are naturally poor, sinful, corrupt men. In a king's palace there is not only a mansion or room of state built for the king himself, and for his eldest son and heir, but there are many rooms, mansions for all his numerous household, children, attendants, and servants.

(3) It is further implied that heaven is a house that was actually built and prepared for a great multitude. When God made heaven in the beginning of the world, He intended it for an everlasting dwelling place for a vast and innumerable multitude. When heaven was made, it was intended and prepared for all those particular persons whom God had from eternity designed to save. Matthew 25:34: "Come, ye blessed of My Father, inherit the kingdom prepared for you from the foundation of the world." And that is a very great and innumerable multitude. Revelation 7:9: "After this I beheld, and, lo, a great multitude which no man could

number, of all nations, and kindreds, and peoples, and tongues, stood before the throne and before the Lamb, clothed with white robes." Heaven, being built designedly for these, was built accordingly; it was built so as most conveniently to accommodate all this multitude, as a house that is built for a great family is built large and with many rooms in it; a palace that is built for a great king that keeps a great court with many attendants is built exceedingly great with a great many apartments; and a house of public worship that is built for a great congregation is built very large with many seats in it.

(4) When it is said, "In My Father's house are many mansions," it is meant that there are seats of various dignity and different degrees and circumstances of honor and happiness. There are many mansions in God's house because heaven is intended for various degrees of honor and blessedness. Some are designed to sit in higher places there than others; some are designed to be advanced to higher degrees of honor and glory than others are. And, therefore, there are various mansions, and some more honorable mansions and seats in heaven than others. Though they are all seats of exceeding honor and blessedness, yet some are more so than others.

Thus a palace is built. Though every part of the palace is magnificent as becomes the palace of a king, yet there are many apartments of various honor, and some are more stately and costly than others, according to the degree of dignity. There is one apartment that is the king's chamber; there are other apartments for the next heir to the crown; there are others for other children; and others for their attendants and the great officers of the household—one for the high steward, another for the chamberlain, and others for meaner officers and servants.

Another image of this was in Solomon's temple. There were many mansions of different degrees of honor and dignity. There was the holy of holies, where the ark was that was the place of God's immediate residence, where the high priest alone might come. There was another apartment called the holy place, where the other priests might come; next to that was the inner court of the temple, where the Levites were admitted; and there they had many chambers or mansions built for lodging rooms for the priests. Next to that was the court of Israel, where the people of Israel might come; and next to that was the court of the Gentiles where the Gentiles, those who were called the "proselytes of the gate," might come.

We have an image of this in houses built for the worship of Christian assemblies. In such houses of God there are many seats of different honor and dignity, from the most honorable to the most inferior of the congregation.

Not that we are to understand the words of Christ so much in a literal sense, as that every saint in heaven was to have a certain seat or room or place of abode where he was to be locally fixed. 'Tis not the design of the Scriptures to inform us much about the external circumstances of heaven, or the state of heaven locally considered; but we are to understand what Christ says chiefly in a spiritual sense. Persons shall be set in different degrees of honor and glory in heaven, as is abundantly manifested in Scripture. This may fitly be represented to our imaginations by there being different seats of honor, as it was in the temple, as it is in kings' courts. Some seats shall be nearer the throne than others. Some shall sit next to Christ in glory. Matthew 20:23: "To sit on My right hand and on My left is not Mine to give, but it shall be given to them for whom it is prepared of My Father."

Christ has respect to these different degrees of glory in the text. When He was going to heaven and the disciples were sorrowful at the thoughts of parting with their Lord, He let them know that there are seats or mansions of various degrees of honor in His Father's house, that there was not only one for Him, who was the Head of the church and the elder Brother, but also for them who were His disciples and younger brethren.

Christ also may probably have respect not only to different degrees of glory in heaven, but different circumstances. Though the employment and happiness of all the heavenly assembly shall in the general be the same, yet 'tis not improbable that there may be circumstantial differences. We know what their employment is in general, but not in particular. We do not know how one may be employed to serve and promote the happiness of another, and all to help one another. Some may there be set in one place for one office or employment, and others in another, as it is in the church on earth. God has set every one in the body as it has pleased Him: one is the eye, another the ear, another the head, and so on. But because God has not been pleased expressly to reveal how it shall be in this respect, therefore I shall not insist upon it here.

Application

Here is encouragement for sinners who are concerned and exercised for the salvation of their souls. Such are afraid that they shall never go to heaven or be admitted to any place of abode there, and are sensible that they are hitherto in a doleful state and condition in that they are out of Christ, and so have no right to any inheritance in heaven, but are in danger of going to hell and having their place of eternal abode fixed there. You may be encouraged by what has been said to earnestly seek heaven, for there are many mansions there. There is room enough there. Let your case be what it will, there is suitable provision there for you; and if you come to Christ, you need not fear that He will not prepare a place for you. He will see to it that you shall be well accommodated in heaven.

But I would apply this doctrine in a twofold exhortation:

1. Let all be hence exhorted earnestly to seek that they may be admitted to a mansion in heaven. You have heard that this is God's house; it is His temple. If David, when he was in the wilderness of Judah and in the land of Geshur and of the Philistines, so longed that he might again return into the land of Israel that he might have a place in the house of God here on earth, and prized a place there so much, though it was but that of a doorkeeper, how great a happiness will it be to have a place in this heavenly temple of God! If they are looked upon as enjoying a high privilege who have a seat appointed them in kings' courts or in apartments in kings' palaces, especially those who have an abode there in the quality of the king's children, then how great a privilege will it be to have an apartment or mansion assigned to us in God's heavenly palace, and to have a place there as His children! How great is their glory and honor who are admitted to be of the household of God!

And seeing there are many mansions there, mansions enough for us all, our folly will be the greater if we neglect to seek a place in heaven, having our minds foolishly taken up about the worthless, fading things of this world. Here consider three things:

(1) Consider how little a time you can have any mansion or place of abode in this world. Now you have a dwelling among the living. You have a house or man-

sion of your own, or at least one that is at present for
your use, and now you have a seat in the house of God;
but how little a while will this continue! In a very little
while, the place that now knows you in this world will
know you no more. The habitation you have here will
be empty of you; you will be carried dead out of it, or
shall die at a distance from it, and never enter into it
any more, or into any other abode in this world. Your
mansion or place of abode in this world, however convenient or commodious it may be, is but as a tent that
shall soon be taken down. Your stay is, as it were, but
for a night. Your body itself is but a house of clay which
will quickly molder and tumble down, and you shall
have no other habitation here in this world but the
grave.

Thus God in His providence is putting you in mind
by the repeated instances of death that have been in the
town within the two weeks past, both in one house. In
these deaths He has shown His dominion over old and
young. The son was taken away first before the father,
being in his full strength and flower of his days; and
the father, who was then well, and having no
appearance of approaching death, followed in a few
days. And their habitation and their seat in the house
of God in this world will know them no more.

Take warning by these warnings of Providence to
improve your time that you may have a mansion in
heaven. We have a house of worship newly created
among us which now you have a seat in, and probably
are pleased with the ornaments of it; and though you
have a place in so comely a house, yet you know not
how little a while you shall have a place in this house of
God. Here are a couple snatched away by death who had
met in it but a few times, who have been snatched out
of it before it was fully finished and never will have any
more a seat in it. You do not know how soon you may

follow, and then it will be of great importance to you to have a seat in God's house above. Both of the persons lately deceased, when on their deathbeds, were warning others to improve their precious time. The first of them was much in expressing his sense of the vast importance of an interest in Christ, as I was a witness, and was earnest in calling on others to improve their time, to be thorough, to get an interest in Christ, and seemed very desirous that young people might receive council and warning from him, as the words of a dying man, to do their utmost to make sure of conversion. A little before he died he left a request with me that I would warn the young people in his place. God has been warning you in his death, and the death of his father that so soon followed. The words of dying persons should be of special weight with us, for then they are in circumstances wherein they are most capable to look on things as they are and judge aright of them.

Let our young people, therefore, take warning from hence, and don't be such fools as to neglect seeking a place and mansion in heaven. Young persons are especially apt to be taken with the pleasing things of this world. You are now, it may be, much pleased with hopes of your future circumstances in this world; and you are now, it may be, much pleased with the ornaments of that house of worship that you with others have a place in. But, alas, do you not too little consider how soon you may be taken away from all these things, and no more forever have any part in any mansion or house or enjoyment or happiness under the sun? Therefore let it be your main care to secure an everlasting habitation for hereafter.

(2) Consider that, when you die, if you have no mansion in the house of God in heaven, you must have your place of abode in the habitation of devils. There is no middle place between them, and when you go

hence, you must go to one or the other of these. Some
have a mansion prepared for them in heaven from the
foundation of the world; others are sent away as cursed
into everlasting burnings prepared for the devil and his
angels. Consider how miserable those must be who
shall have their habitation with devils to all eternity.
Devils are foul spirits, God's great enemies. Their habitation is the blackness of darkness, a place of the utmost filthiness, abomination, darkness, disgrace and
torment. Oh, would you not rather ten thousand times
have no place of abode at all, have no being at all, than
to have a place with devils!

(3) If you die unconverted, you will have the
worse place in hell for having had a seat or place in
God's house in this world. As there are many mansions,
places of different degrees of honor in heaven, so there
are various abodes and places or degrees of torment
and misery in hell; and those will have the worst place
there who, dying unconverted, have had the best place
in God's house here. Solomon speaks of a peculiarly
awful sight that he had seen of a wicked man buried
who had gone from the place of the holy (Ecclesiastes
8:10.) Such as have had a seat in God's house have been,
in a sense, exalted up to heaven, set on the gate of
heaven; if they die unconverted, they shall be cast down
to hell.

2. The second exhortation that I would offer from
what has been said is to seek a high place in heaven.
Seeing that there are many mansions of different degrees of honor and dignity in heaven, let us seek to obtain a mansion of distinguished glory. 'Tis revealed to
us that there are different degrees of glory to the end
that we might seek after the higher degrees. God offered high degrees of glory to the end that we might
seek them by eminent holiness and good works.
2 Corinthians 9:6: "He that sows sparingly shall reap

also sparingly; and he that soweth bountifully shall reap also bountifully." It is not becoming persons to be over- anxious about a high seat in God's house in this world, for that is the honor that is from men; but we can't too earnestly seek after a high seat in God's house above by seeking eminent holiness, for that is the honor that is from God.

'Tis very little worth the time for us to pursue after honor in this world, where the greatest honor is but a bubble and will soon vanish away, and death will level all. Some have more stately houses than others, some are in higher office than others, some are richer than others, and have higher seats in the meeting house than others, but all graves are upon a level. One rotting, putrefying corpse is as ignoble as another; the worms are as bold with one carcass as another.

But the mansions in God's house above are everlasting mansions. Those who have seats allotted to them there, whether of greater or lesser dignity, whether nearer or further from the throne, will hold them to all eternity. This is promised in Revelation 3:12: "Him that overcometh I will make him a pillar in the temple of My God, and he shall go no more out." If it is worthwhile to desire and seek high seats in the meeting house, where you are one day in a week, and where you shall never come but few days in all; if it is worthwhile much to prize one seat above another in the house of worship, only because it is the pew or seat that is ranked first in number, and to be seen here for a few days, how worthwhile will it be to seek a high mansion in God's temple, and in that glorious place that is the everlasting habitation of God and all His children! You who are pleased with your seats in this house because you are seated high, or in a place that is looked upon as honorable by those who sit round about, and because many can behold you, consider how short a time you will enjoy this pleasure. And if there are any who are not suited in their seats because they are too low for them, let them consider that it is but a very little while before it will be all one to you whether you have sat high or low here. But it will be of infinite and everlasting concern to you where your seat is in another world.

Let your great concern be, while in this world, so to improve your opportunities in God's house in this world, whether you sit high or low, as that you may have a distinguished and glorious mansion in God's house in heaven, where you may be fixed in your place in that glorious assembly in an everlasting rest.

Let the main thing that we prize in God's house be not the outward ornaments of it, or a high seat in it, but the Word of God and His ordinances in it. Spend your time here seeking Christ, that He may prepare a place for you in His Father's house, so that when He comes again to this world, He may take you to Himself, so that where He is, there you may be also.